ALMUT HINTZE · ZAMYĀD YAŠT

Zamyād Yašt

Introduction, Avestan Text, Translation, Glossary

by

ALMUT HINTZE

WIESBADEN 1994

DR. LUDWIG REICHERT VERLAG

CIP-Einheitsaufnahme der Deutschen Bibliothek

Zamyād Yašt : introduction, Avestan text, translation, glossary
/ by Almut Hintze. -
Wiesbaden : Reichert 1994
ISBN 3-88226-785-2
NE: Hintze, Almut [Hrsg.]

Contents

નાદીરને
મિત્રટાની સાથે

Preface

The text and translation of the Zamyād Yašt published here is based on my more comprehensive and detailed work in German, *Der Zamyād-Yašt*. Edition, Übersetzung, Kommentar. Wiesbaden: Dr. Ludwig Reichert Verlag, 1994, which is a revised version of my doctoral dissertation directed by Professor Johanna Narten at Erlangen University. For discussion of individual passages in the text as well as the justification of the translation the reader is referred to that book.

In that work, the text and translation of the Zamyād Yašt is split up into individual stanzas, so that the reader finds, for each stanza, the Avestan text, variant readings, translation and commentary in one place. However, it seemed useful also to have a version in which the text runs continuously for the benefit of the reader who wishes to get a general idea of the text. In order to make the translation more accessible to the general reader, and to members of the Zoroastrian community in particular, the language chosen for the translation here is English. The glossary is intended to be of assistance to students wishing to embark upon the study of the Avestan language.

I am very grateful to Dr. Elizabeth Tucker, one of my teachers from Oxford University, for kindly looking through the manuscript of this book at various stages and giving me valuable suggestions about the English translation and the glossary. Mr Farrokh Jal Vajifdar (London) has given me useful hints, too. I would also like to thank my friend Nadir Godrej (Bombay) for making the translation more poetic. To him this little book is dedicated.

It is hoped that this booklet may prove useful to students of the Avestan language and to friends and followers of Zarathushtra's religion.

Almut Hintze

Berlin, September 1994

Introduction

The Zamyād Yašt (= Yašt 19) is a hymn (MP *yašt* 'prayer, worship') that forms part of the text corpus called the Avesta, the holy texts of the Mazdayasnians, who follow the religion founded by their prophet Zarathushtra. The language of these texts is an old North–East Iranian dialect of which, however, no documents outside the Avesta have been preserved. The language of the Avesta is therefore simply called Avestan.

The date of the Avestan texts and the date of Zarathushtra's lifetime is difficult to establish and much disputed among scholars. However, there is at least a consensus that the texts belonging to the Avesta are not all from the same time but date from different periods. This can be seen from the language, which reflects a later stage of development in some of the texts than in others, as well as from the contents of the texts, since the texts do not represent a uniform stage of development of the religion.

The oldest parts of the Avesta are embedded in the middle of the 72 chapters of the Yasna ('worship'). The recitation of the Yasna accompanies the preparation and offering of the juice of the Haoma–plant mixed with sacrificial water, milk and other ingredients, but the text recited stands only partly in relationship to the ritual action. The oldest parts of the Avesta are called the Gāthās ('songs') and the authorship of these 17 songs is attributed by indigenous tradition as well as by most Avestan scholars to Zarathushtra himself. The Gāthās themselves enclose in their middle the Yasna Haptaŋhāiti ('worship in seven chapters'), the very centre of the Yasna–ceremony. The language of the Gāthās, the Yasna Haptaŋhāiti and four holy prayers (Y 27.13 *Ahuna Vairiia*, Y 27.14 *Aṣ̌əm vohū*, Y 27.15 *Yeŋhē hātąm*, Y 54.1 *Airiiaman Išiia*) is called Old Avestan, because the language of these texts is more archaic than the language of the rest of the Avesta, which is called Young Avestan.

The text corpus of the Younger Avesta is much larger than that of the Older Avesta. In addition to the remaining chapters of the Yasna, to the Younger Avesta belong the Vispered, the Vīdēvdād, some minor texts such as the Niyāyišns, Gāhs, Sīrōza and Āfrīngāns, and the Yašts. The 24 chapters of the Visperad (from Av. *vīspe ratauuō* 'all the Ratus') are liturgical texts which are inserted into the Yasna in the Yasna–ceremony. The Vīdēvdād (Av. *vī–daēuua-dāta-* 'law of those who reject the Daēvas')[1] contains purity laws in 22 chapters. This text gives valuable insight into the private life of Mazdayasnians of the post–Achaemenian period. The five Niyāyišns are texts of praise and prayers to various Yazatas ('venerable ones'). The Gāhs are the five prayers each to be recited at a certain time of the day. Each of the two Sīrōzas contains a list of the thirty days of the month named after the Yazatas who are praised on the individual days. The Āfrīngāns are blessings pronounced on various occasions.

---

[1] On the meaning of the name see BENVENISTE, "Que signifie Vidēvdāt?". *Henning Memorial Volume*, London 1970, 37–42.

A substantial and important part of the Younger Avesta is constituted by the 21 resp. 22 Yašts[2]. These are hymns not only to Ahura Mazdā, the highest god, but also to various other Yazatas. In fact, the hymns to Ahura Mazdā (Yt 1), to the Aməša Spəntas (Yt 2), Aša Vahišta (Yt 3) and Haurvatāt (Yt 4) are rather short and formulaic compilations compared to the longer and more original hymns to Anāhitā (Yt 5), Tištrya (Yt 8), Mithra (Yt 10), the Fravašis (Yt 13), Vərəθraγna (Yt 14), Aši Vaη^vhī (Yt 17) and Zamyād (Yt 19). Each Yašt is attributed to a certain day of the month whose genius is praised in the respective Yašt. The order of the Yašts corresponds to the order of the days of the month as it is fixed in the Sīrōza.

In spite of the fact that it has not been possible to reconstruct a metrical pattern which is applied with consistency in the Yašts, the Yašts seem to be metrical poetry. This emerges from a definite preponderance of verse–lines counting eight syllables. Thus, for instance, in the Zamyād Yašt a whole series of stanzas consists of eight–syllabic verses, e.g. Yt 19.92–96. The numerous exceptions from the regular eight– or twelve–syllabic verse may be explained in that the original metrical pattern has not been preserved consistently in the text–form of the Yašts which has come down to us.

The Zamyād Yašt is attributed to the 28th day of the month, the day of the Earth. From this the Yašt has its name (Av. *zam-* 'earth'). However, only a very small portion of the Zamyād Yašt deals with the earth and even that part is not a proper hymn with an opening and closing formula of praise, but much more a list of names of mountains found in the land of the Iranians. The first and the last stanza of the section on the earth are narratives telling about the primordial mountains, the lofty Haraitī and the Zərəδaza–mountain (stanza 1), out of which all other mountains, whose names are given in stanzas 2–6 and which number 2244 (stanza 7), were to arise. The last stanza of that section tells how the land, over which these mountains extend, was divided among the three social groups, namely the priests, the warriors and the farmers (stanza 8).

It is only from stanza 9 of the Zamyād Yašt that the proper hymn starts, but it is not the Earth that is being praised but the *x^varənah-* (MP *xwarrah* 'fortune, glory, splendour'). The praise of the *x^varənah-* is the proper theme of the Zamyād Yašt and it continues throughout the hymn until the end in stanza 96. One gets the impression that stanza 9–96 form an independent hymn to *x^varənah-* which was only combined with stanza 1–8, the section on the Earth, in order that the whole Yašt might be attributed to the day of the Earth, the 28th day of the month, because the *x^varənah-* does not have its own day in the Mazdayasnian calendar.

The hymn to *x^varənah-*, i.e. stanza 9–96 of the Zamyād Yašt, deals with divine and human beings who owned or desired the *x^varənah-*, and tells what they did

---

[2] The number of Yašts depends on whether the Srōš Yašt transmitted in the Yasna (Y 57 = Yt 11a) is counted as one of the Yašts.

when they possessed the x^v*arənah*- or what they did in order to get hold of it. Two types of x^v*arənah*- are distinguished in that hymn: the x^v*arənah*- belonging to the Kauui–dynasty (Av. *kauuaēm* x^v*arənō*) and the gleaming x^v*arənah*- (Av. *ax^{v}arətəm* x^v*arənō*). The x^v*arənah*- of the Kauui–dynasty belonged to Ahura Mazdā when he created the world, to the Aməša Spəntas, to all other Yazatas and the Renovators and Saviours (stanza 9–24). Furthermore, it accompanied the Rulers of the Peš-dadian dynasty, Haošiiaŋha, Urupi.azinauuaṇt and Yima. But Yima lost the x^v*arənah*-, because he had started to lie. Along with the x^v*arənah*- Yima also lost his rule and kingdom and started to wander about on the earth unhappily. The x^v*arənah*- left Yima three times in the shape of a bird of prey and each time it flew away it was grasped in turn by Mithra and the heroes Thraētaona and Kərəsāspa. The references to the names of the heroes gives an opportunity to the poets to tell stories about their heroic feats, especially their slaying of the dragon (26–44).

The praise of the gleaming x^v*arənah*- forms the centre of the hymn (stanza 45–69). The gleaming x^v*arənah*- does not accompany divine and human beings but is desired by them. Spəṇta Mainiiu and Aŋra Mainiiu desire it and send out their swiftest messengers to catch it. There is a description of the race between the Fire and the Dragon Dahāka, each of whom wants to get hold of the x^v*arənah*-, but just as one of them wants to grab it, he is frightened by the threatening words of his adversary. The x^v*arənah*- escapes to Lake Vourukaša and at the bottom of the deep lake the Yazata, the Lord Apəm Napāt, grabs it (45–54). Then the Turanian Fraŋrasiian comes along to the lake wanting to catch the x^v*arənah*-. He throws off his clothes and jumps naked into the water trying to grasp the x^v*arənah*-. But the x^v*arənah*- escapes and at the place to which it has escaped a new bay emerges. Very angry Fraŋrasiian comes out of the water speaking words of abuse. Then he starts a second and a third attempt, which are described in the same way and remain likewise without success. With each failed attempt Fraŋrasiian speaks more words of abuse (55–64). This is followed by a description of the region of Lake Kạsaoiia and the Haētumaṇt, which is full of x^v*arənah*- (65–69).

In the remaining part of the hymn it is again the x^v*arənah*- of the Kauui–dynasty that is praised. The x^v*arənah*- of the Kauui–dynasty accompanied the individual rulers of that dynasty whose names are listed, especially Kauui Hao-srauuah, who defeated the Turanian Fraŋrasiian (70–77). The x^v*arənah*- of the Kauui–dynasty also accompanied Zarathushtra so that he could think, speak and act according to the religion and, with the help of the Ahuna–Vairiia–prayer, chase all demons under the earth. It is this x^v*arənah*- which accompanied Kauui Vīštāspa so that he could defeat all enemies of the new religion (78–87). Finally, the x^v*arənah*- of the Kauui–dynasty accompanies the 'victorious one among the saviours' (Yt 19.89 *saošiiaṇtəm vərəϑrājanəm*), that is Astuuaṭ.ərəta, and his friends, when he brings about the renovation of the world (Av. *frašō.kərə-ti*-). Astuuaṭ.ərəta, the son of Vīspa.tauruuairī, steps forth from Lake Kạsaoiia brandishing his victorious missile, his gaze making the whole corporeal world indestructible. Aŋra Mainiiu is completely defeated and retreats powerless (88–96).

This last section describing the renovation of the world is unique in the whole of the Avesta, since it is the most detailed description of the eschatological events that has come down to us. Apart from this, the Zamyād Yašt contains also other unique and original passages, such as the description of the contest between the Fire and Aži Dahāka, or the episode of the three failed attempts of the Turanian Fraŋrasiian to get hold of the gleaming $x^v ar \partial nah$-. The detailed geographical description of the region of the Haētumaṇt is unique in the Avesta, too. This hymn contains several pearls of Avestan literature which render it well worth reading.

Zamyād Yašt

Avestan Text[3] and Translation

1. *paoiriiō̆ gairiš həm.hištaṯ*[1]   'The first mountain to arise,
   spitama zaraϑuštra   o Spitāma Zaraϑuštra,
   paiti āiia zəmā[1a] *haraiti barš*   on this earth (was) the lofty Haraitī;
   hā hama ×*pairi.saēte*[2]   the whole of it extends around
   frāpaiiā̊[3] *daŋhūš*[4] *ā*   both up to the western lands and
   ×*upaošaŋⁿʰå̄sca*[5]   (up to) the eastern (lands).
   bitiiō̆[5a] *zərəδazō*[6] *gairiš*   The second mountain (to arise was)
   pārəṇtarəm[7] *arəδō̆*[7a] *manušahe*   Zərəδaza, the other half of Manuša;
   hāmō hasciṯ ×*pairi.saēte*[2a]   the whole of it extends around
   frāpaiiā̊[3a] *daŋhūš*[4a] *ā*   both up to the western lands and
   ×*upaošaŋⁿʰå̄sca*[5b]   (up to) the eastern (lands).'

2. *ahmaṯ haca garaiiō̆ fraoxšiiąn*   'From there grew forth the mountains:
   ×*usaδā̊*[1] *ušidarəno*   Usaδā Ušidarəna
   ərəzifiiasca[1a] *fraorəpō*   and the mountain Ǝrəzifiia,
   xštuuō[1b] *ərəzurō*[2]   as the sixth Ǝrəzura,
   haptaϑō̆[2a] *būmiiō*[3]   as the seventh Būmiia,
   aštəmō[3a] *raoδitō*   as the eighth Raoδita,
   naomō[4] *mazišuuā̊*[5]   as the ninth Mazišuuaṇt,
   dasəmō aṇtarə.daŋhuš[6]   as the tenth Aṇtarə.daŋhu,
   aēuuaṇdasō ərəzišō[7]   as the eleventh Ǝrəziša,
   duuadasō[7a] *vāiti.gaēsō*[8]   as the twelfth Vāiti.gaēsa;'

3. *ādaranasca*[1] *baiianasca*   'and Ādarana and Baiiana,
   iškatāca[2] *upāiri.saēna*[3]   and Iškata Upāiri.saēna,
   kạsō.tafəδra[4] +*vafra*[5]   Kạsō.tafəδrā (and) Vafrā,
   duua hamaṇkuna[5a] *pauruuata*   the two rocky mountains hooked
   ašta.vašano[5b.6] *pauruuata*   together, the Eight–Pass mountains,
   ašta.auruuaṇtō[6a.7] ×*frą̄kauuō*[8]   the Eight–Runner peaks,
   caϑβārō viδβana[9] *kaofō*   the Four–Viδβana mountains.'

---

[3] The numbers following individual Avestan words indicate that there are variant readings in the manuscripts. The numbers are identical with those in my critical edition of the text.

4. *aēzaxasca*[1] *maēnaxasca*[1b]
   vāxəδrikaēca[2] *asaiiaēca*[3]
   tuδaskaēca[4] *višauuaēca*[5]
   draošišuuåsca[6] *sāiriuuåsca*
   naŋhušmåsca[7] *kakahiiušca*[8]
   aṇtarə.kaŋhaca[9]

   'Aēzaxa and Maēnaxa,
   the two Vāxəδrikā and the two Asaiiā,
   the two Tuδaskā and the two Višauuā,
   Draošišuuaṇt and Sāiriuuaṇt,
   Naŋhušmaṇt and Kakahiiu
   and the Aṇtarə.kaŋha(–mountains).'

5. [×]*sicidāuuasca*[1] *ahuranasca*[2]
   raēmanasca[2a] *aša.stəmbanasca*[3]
   uruṅiiō.vāiδimiδkaēca[4]
   [×]*asanuuåsca*[5] [×]*usaomasca*[6]
   *ušta.x*ᵛ*arənåsca siiāmakasca*[7]
   [×]*vafrauuåsca*[7a] *vourušasca*[8]

   'Sicidauua and Ahurana,
   Raēmana and Aša.stəmbana
   and the two Uruṅiiō.vāiδimiδkā,
   Asanuuaṇt and Usaoma,
   Ušta.xᵛarənah and Siiāmaka,
   Vafrauuaṇt and Vouruša.'

6. *yahmiia.jatarasca*[1] *aδutauuåsca*[2]
   spitauuarənåsca[3] *spəṇtō.dātasca*
   kadruua.aspasca[3a] *kaoirisasca*[4]
   taērasca barō.sraiianō[4a]
   baranasca[5] *frāpaiiåsca gairiš*
   [6]*udriiasca raēuuåsca gairiš*[6]
   yaēšəmca[6a] *parō mašiiāka*[6b]
   [+]*aiβitaēδca*[7] [+]*spašitaēδca*[8]
   gairinąm[8a] *nāmąm*[9] *dāδarə*

   'Yahmiia.jatara and Aδutauuah,
   Spitauuarənah and Spəṇtō.dāta,
   Kadruua.aspa and Kaoirisa,
   and the peak of Barō.sraiian,
   Barana and the mountain Frāpaiiah,
   Udriia and the mountain Raēuuaṇt,
   and the other mountains to whom
   the mortals have given names formerly
   (taking them) from walking on and ob-
   serving (the mountains).'

7. *caϑβarasca*[1a] *aϑa garaiiō*
   spitama zaraϑuštra
   caϑβarəsatəmca[1b] *duuaēca*[1] *saite*
   duuaēca[1] *hazaŋre*

   'Thus there are,
   o Spitāma Zaraϑuštra,
   two thousand and two hundred
   and forty–four mountains.'

8. *yauuat anu aipi*
   [×]*aēte*[1] *garaiiō višastarə*[2]
   vīspəm[2a] *auuat aipi draonō bažat*[3]
   aϑ aurunaēca[3a] *raϑ aēštāica*[3b]
   vāstriiāica[3c] *fšuiieṇte*[3d]

   'Over all this space
   over which these mountains extend
   the share for the priest, the warrior
   and for the farmer who breeds cattle
   has been established.'

Karde I

9. *uγrəm kauuaēm x^{v}arənō*
   mazdaδātəm yazamaide
   aš.vandrəm[1] uparō.kairīm
   ϑamnaŋ^{v}hantəm[2] varəcaŋ^{v}hantəm[3]
   yaoxštiuuantəm
   taraδātəm[4] añiiāiš dāmąn

'We worship the mighty Glory of the Kauui-dynasty created by Mazdā, the highly praised, supreme worker, determined, energetic, skilful, overcoming the other creatures.'

10. *yaṯ asti ahurahe mazdā̊*
    yaϑa dāmąn daϑaṯ ahurō mazdā̊
    pouruca vohuca pouruca srīraca
    pouruca abdaca[1] pouruca frašaca
    pouruca bāmiiāca[1a]

'(The Glory,) which belongs to Ahura Mazdā, so that Ahura Mazdā creates the creatures, the many good ones, the many beautiful ones, the many marvellous ones, the many excellent ones, the many radiant ones.'

11. *yaṯ kərənauuąn [1]frašəm ahum[1a]*
    [+]azarəsəntəm[2] [+]amarəśantəm[3]
    afriϑiiantəm apuiiantəm[3a]
    yauuaējīm[4] yauuaēsūm[4a]
    vasō.xšaϑrəm
    yaṯ irista[4b] paiti usəhištən
    jasāṯ juuaiiō[5] amərəxtiš
    daϑaite[6] frašəm vasna[7] aŋhuš

'So that they may make life excellent, ageless, without decay, not rotting, not putrefying, living forever, thriving forever, ruling as it wishes. When the dead will rise, (then) will come the one without decay reviving (the dead) (and) life will create excellent things according to its own wish.'

12. *būn[1] gaēϑā̊ amaršantīš[2]*
    yā̊ ašahe saŋ^{v}haitīš
    [+]niš [+]taṯ[3] paiti druxš nāšāite[4]
    yaδāṯ aiβiciṯ jaγmaṯ
    ašauuanəm mahrkaϑāi
    aom ciϑrəmca[5] stimca[6]
    āϑaṯca[7] ×maire[7a.8] nāšātaēca[8]
    mairiiō[9] aϑa[10] ×aratuš[10a]

'The world of Truth will be undecaying from generation to generation. Falsehood will be returned to the place where it had come from to destroy the truthful one, himself, his family and existence. The (female) villain will be terrified and the lawless (male) villain will disappear.'

13. *[1a]ahe raiia x^{v}arənaŋhaca*
    təm[1b] yazāi surunuuata yasna[1]

'On account of his splendour and glory I will worship him with audible venera-

uγrəm kauuaēm x^{v}arənō
mazdaδātəm zaoϑrābiiō
uγrəm kauuaēm x^{v}arənō
  mazdaδātəm yazamaide
  $^+$haoma^2 $^+$yō^2 gauua
  [= Ny 1,16 barəsmana
  hizuuō^4 daŋhaŋha^5 m$ə̨$ϑraca
  vacaca śiiaoϑnaca zaoϑrābiiasca
  aršuxδaēbiiasca vāγžibiiō^6
^{7}yeńhē hātąm āaṱ yesnē paitī
vaŋhō^8 mazdå̄ ahurō vaēϑā
ašāṱ hacā yåŋhąmcā
tąscā] tåscā yazamaide

tion, the mighty Glory of the Kauui–
dynasty, created by Mazdā (I will worship him) with libations. We worship
the mighty Glory of the Kauui–dynasty,
created by Mazdā with Haoma mixed
with milk, with sacrificial grass,
with skill of tongue and formulation,
with word and deed, and with libations
and with correctly uttered words.
In the worship of which (male Entities) of those who exist and in the worship of which (female Entities) the Wise
Lord knows what is better according
to Truth, we worship these (male) and
these (female Entities).'

Karde II

14. uγrəm kauuaēm x^{v}arənō
  mazdaδātəm yazamaide
  aš.vaṇdrəm^1 uparō.kairīm
  ϑamnaŋ^{v}haṇtəm^2 varəcaŋ^{v}haṇtəm^3
    yaoxštiuuaṇtəm
  taraδātəm^4 ańiiāiš dāmąn

'We worship the mighty Glory of the
Kauui–dynasty created by Mazdā,
the highly praised, supreme worker,
determined, energetic,
  skilful,
overcoming the other creatures.'

15. yaṱ asti ^{1}aməšanąm spəṇtanąm
  xšaētanąm $^×$varəzi.dōiϑranąm^{1a}
  $^×$bərəzatąm^2 aiβiiāmanąm^3
  taxmanąm āhūiriianąm
  yōi aiϑiiejaŋhō^4 ašauuanō

'Which belongs to the Incremental Im-
mortals, the shining ones, whose eyes
are powerful, the lofty, aggressive ones,
the brave, lordly ones, who are
free from danger, the truthful ones.'

16. ^{1a}yōi hapta hamō.manaŋhō
yōi hapta hamō.vacaŋhō
yōi hapta hamō.śiiaoϑnåŋhō
yaēšąm^{1b} asti haməm manō
  haməm vacō haməm śiiaoϑnəm
  hamō $^+$ptāca^1 frasāstaca^{1c}
  yō daδuuå̊ ahurō mazdå̄^{2}

'The seven, who think alike,
the seven, who speak alike,
the seven, who act alike.
Who have the same thought,
the same word, the same deed,
the same father and master,
the creator Ahura Mazdā.'

17. yaēšąm ańiiō ańiiehe[1b]
     uruuānəm aiβi.vaēnaiti[1]
     mərəϑβəntəm[2] humataēšu
     mərəϑβəntəm[2] hūxtaēšu
     mərəϑβəntəm[2] huuarštaēšu
     mərəϑβəntəm[2] garō nmānəm[2a]
  yaēšąm raoxšną̊ŋhō paṇtānō
     āuuaiiatąm auui zaoϑrą̊

'Of whom one looks upon
the soul of the other,
while thinking of good thoughts,
while thinking of good words,
while thinking of good deeds,
while thinking of the House of Welcome.
Whose paths are light
when they draw near to the libations.'

18. yōi həṇti ą̊ŋhąm dāmanąm
     yat ahurahe mazdā̊
     dātarasca marəxštarasca[1a]
     ϑβarəxštarasca aiβiiāxštarasca
     nipātarasca[1b] nišharətarasca[1]

'Who are the creators and formers,
the fashioners and guardians,
the protectors and watchers
of these creatures
of Ahura Mazdā.'

19. taēcit yōi vasna frašəm ahum daϑən
     +azarəsəṇtəm[1] +amarəšáṇtəm[2]
     afriϑiiaṇtəm apuiiaṇtəm
     [(= Yt 19.11) yauuaējīm[4]
         yauuaēsūm[4a] vasō.xšaϑrəm
  yat irista[4b] paiti usəhištąn
     jasāt juuaiiō[5] amərəxtiš
     daϑaite[6] frašəm vasna[7] aŋhuš]

'It is they who will make life excellent
according to wish, ageless, without
decay, not rotting, not putrefying,
living forever, thriving forever,
    ruling as it wishes.
When the dead will rise, (then) will
come the one without decay reviving
(the dead) (and) life will create excellent things according to its own wish.'

20. [(= Yt 19.12) būn[1] gaēϑą̊
         amarəšáṇtīš[2]
     yą̊ ašahe saŋ^vhaitīš
     +niš +tat[3] paiti druxš nāšāite[4]
     yaδāt aiβicit jaγmat
  ašauuanəm mahrkaϑāi
     aom ciϑrəmca[5] stīmca[6]
  āϑ atca[7] ×maire[7a.8] nāšātaēca[8]
     mairiiō[9] aϑa[10] ×aratuš[10a]]
  ahe raiia ... (= Yt 19.13)...
  ... tā̊scā yazamaide

'The world of Truth will be
         undecaying
from generation to generation.
Falsehood will be returned to the place
where it had come from
to destroy the truthful one, himself, his
family and existence. The (female) villain will be terrified and the lawless
(male) villain will disappear.'
On account of his splendour ...
and these (female Entities) we worship.'

Karde III

21. *uγrəm kauuaēm* [(= Yt 19.9)
    x^{v}arənō
    mazdaδātəm yazamaide
    aš.vaṇdrəm uparō.kairīm
    ϑamnaη^{v}haṇtəm varəcaη^{v}haṇtəm
      yaoxštiuuaṇtəm]
    taraδātəm^{1a} aṅiiāiš dāmąn

          'We worship the mighty Glory
            of the Kauui–dynasty
          created by Mazdā,
          the highly praised, supreme worker,
          determined, energetic,
            skilful,
          overcoming the other creatures.'

22. *yaṱ asti maṅiiauuanąm*
    yazatanąm gaēiϑiianąmca
    zātanąmca azātanąmca^1
    frašō.carəϑrąm saošiiaṇtąmca

          '(The Glory,) which belongs to the
          spiritual and corporeal adorable ones,
          the born and unborn
          Renovators and Saviours.'

23. *taēciṱ yōi frašəm vasna ahum daϑən*
    $^+$*azarəsəṇtəm^1 $^+$amarəšaṇtəm^2*
    afriϑiiaṇtəm apuiiaṇtəm^3
    [(= Yt 19.11) *yauuaējīm^4*
      yauuaēsūm^{4a} vasō.xšaϑrəm
    yaṱ irista^{4b} paiti usəhištąn
      jasāṱ juuaiiō^5 amərəxtiš
      daϑaite^6 frašəm vasna^7 ˌaηhuš]

          'It is they who will make life excellent
          according to wish, ageless, without
          decay, not rotting, not putrefying,
          living forever, thriving forever,
            ruling as it wishes.
          When the dead will rise, (then) will
          come the one without decay reviving
          (the dead) (and) life will create excel-
          lent things according to its own wish.'

24. [(= Yt 19.12) *būn^1 gaēϑå*
      amaršȧṇtīš^2
    yå ašahe saη^{v}haitīš
    $^+$*niš $^+$taṱ^3 paiti druxš nāšāite^4*
    yaδāṱ aiβiciṱ jaγmaṱ
    ašauuanəm mahrkaϑāi
      aom ciϑrəmca^5 stīmca^6
    āϑaṱca^7 $^×$maire$^{7a.8}$ nāšātaēca^8
      mairiiō^9 aϑa^{10} $^×$aratuš^{10a}]
    ahe raiia (= Yt 19.13) ...
    ... *tåscā yazamaide*

          'The world of Truth will be
            undecaying
          from generation to generation.
          Falsehood will be returned to the place
          where it had come from
          to destroy the truthful one, himself, his
          family and existence. The (female) vil-
          lain will be terrified and the lawless
          (male) villain will disappear.'
          On account of his splendour ...
          and these (female Entities) we worship.'

Karde IV

25. *uγrəm kauuaēm* [(= Yt 19.9)   'We worship the mighty Glory
    x^{v}arənō   of the Kauui–dynasty

    mazdaδātəm yazamaide   created by Mazdā,

    aš.vandrəm[1] uparō.kairīm   the highly praised, supreme worker,

    ϑamnaŋ^{v}hantəm[2] varəcaŋ^{v}hantəm[3]   determined, energetic,
    yaoxštiuuantəm   skilful,

    taraδātəm[4]] *ańiiāiš dāmąn*   overcoming the other creatures.'

26. *yat̰ upaŋhacat̰ haošiiaŋhəm[1]*   '(The Glory,) which accompanied
    paraδātəm   Haošiiaŋha Paraδāta,

    darəγəmcit̰ aipi[2] zruuānəm   for a long time,

    yat̰ xšaiiata paiti būmīm haptaiϑiiąm   so that he ruled over the earth of seven

    daēuuanąm mašiiānąmca   parts, over demons and mortals,

    yāϑβąm pairikanąmca   over wizards and witches,

    sāϑrąm kaoiiąm karafnąmca   over commanders, seers and ritualists.

    yō janat̰ duua ϑrišuua   Who slew two thirds

    māzańiianąm daēuuanąm   of the gigantic demons, of the deceitful

    varəńiianąmca druuatąm   ones who have made their (bad) choice.

    ahe raiia ... (= Yt 19.13) ...   On account of his splendour ...

    ... tā̊scā yazamaide   and these (female Entities) we worship.'

Karde V

27. *uγrəm kauuaēm* [(= Yt 19.9)   'We worship the mighty Glory
    x^{v}arənō   of the Kauui–dynasty

    mazdaδātəm yazamaide   created by Mazdā,

    aš.vandrəm[1] uparō.kairīm   the highly praised, supreme worker,

    ϑamnaŋ^{v}hantəm[2] varəcaŋ^{v}hantəm[3]   determined, energetic,
    yaoxštiuuantəm   skilful,

    taraδātəm[4]] *ańiiāiš dāmąn*   overcoming the other creatures.'

28. *yat̰ upaŋhacat̰ taxməm*   'Which accompanied the brave
    urupi.azinauuantəm[1.2.]   Urupi.azinauuaṇt,

    yat̰ xšaiiata paiti būmīm haptaiϑiiąm   so that he ruled over the earth of

    daēuuanąm mašiiānąmca   seven parts, over demons and mortals,

yāϑβąm pairikanąmca	over wizards and witches,
sāϑrąm kaoiiąm karafnąmca	over commanders, seers and ritualists.'

29. yat̰ bauuat̰ aiβi.vaniiā̊   'So that he overcame
    vīspe daēuua mašiiāca   all demons and mortals,
    vīspe yātauuō pairikā̊sca   all wizards and witches.
    yat̰ barata aŋrəm¹ mańiium   (It accompanied him) when he rode the
    framitəm aspahe kəhrpa   Evil Spirit transformed into the shape
    ϑrisatəm aiβi.gāmanąm   of a horse, for thirty years
    uua² pairi zəmō karana   around both edges of the earth.
    ahe raiia ... (= Yt 19.13) ... On account of his splendour ...
    ... tā̊scā yazamaide   and these (female Entities) we worship.'

Karde VI

30. uγrəm kauuaēm [(= Yt 19.9)   'We worship the mighty Glory of the
        xᵛarənō   Kauui–dynasty
    mazdaδātəm yazamaide   created by Mazdā,
    aš.vaṇdrəm¹ uparō.kairīm   the highly praised, supreme worker,
    ϑamnaŋᵛhaṇtəm² varəcaŋᵛhaṇtəm³ determined, energetic,
        yaoxštiuuaṇtəm   skilful,
    taraδātəm⁴] ańiiāiš dāmąn   overcoming the other creatures.'

31. yat̰ upaŋhacat̰¹ᵃ yim yiməm¹ᵇ   '(The Glory,) which accompanied
        xšaētəm¹ᶜ huuąϑβəm¹ᵈ   shining Yima of good herds
    darəγəmcit̰ aipi zruuānəm¹ᵉ   for a long time,
    yat̰ xšaiiata¹ᶠ paiti būmīm¹ᵍ   so that he ruled over the earth
        haptaiϑiiąm¹ʰ   of seven parts,
    daēuuanąm [(= Yt 19.26)   over demons
        mašiiānąmca   and mortals
    yāϑβąm pairikanąmca   over wizards and witches,
    sāϑrąm¹ˡ kaoiiąm] karafnąmca¹ᵐ over commanders, seers and ritualists.'

32. ¹ᵃyō uzbarat̰¹ᵇ haca¹ daēuuaēibiiō² 'Who brought up from the demons
    uiie ištišca³ saokāca³ᵃ   both prosperity and reputation,
    uiie fšaonišca⁴ vąϑβāca   both flocks and herds,

uiie [×]θ*rąfšca*[5] *frasastišca*[6]   both contentment and honour.

yeŋhe[6a] *xšaθrāδa*[7] [×] *x*ⁿ*airiiəm*[8]   Under whose reign let that which is
⁺*tū*[8] *astu*[9]   edible exist:

uiie *x*ⁿ*arəθe*[10] *ajiiamne*[11]   (let) both kinds of the food (be) undi-

amarəšąṇta[12] *pasu.vīra*[12a]   minishing, cattle and men undecaying,

aŋhaošəmne[13] *āpa.uruuaire*[13a]   water and plants not drying up.'

33. *yeŋhe*[1a] *xšaθrāδa*[1]   'Under whose reign

nōiṯ[1b] *aotəm*[1c] åŋha nōiṯ *garəməm*[1d]   there was no frost, no heat,

nōiṯ *zauruua*[1e] åŋha[1e] *nōiṯ*   no old age, no
    mərəiθiiuš[1f]   death,

nōiṯ *araskō*[2] *daēuuō.dātō*[2a]   no envy created by demons:

para anādruxtōiṯ[3]   before his not–lying[4],

para ahmāṯ yaṯ hīm[4] *aēm*   before he took up

   draoγəm[5] *vācim*[5a] *aŋhaiθīm*[5b]   the false word, the untrue one

cinmāne paiti.barata[6]   into his endeavour.'

34. *āaṯ yaṯ hīm*[1] *aēm*[1a]   'When he had taken up

   draoγəm[2] *vācim*[2a] *aŋhaiθīm*[2b]   this false word, the untrue one,

cinmāne[3] *paiti.barata*[4]   into his endeavour,

vaēnəmnəm[4a] *ahmaṯ*[5] *haca x*ⁿ*arənō*   the Glory flew away from him visibly

   mərəγahe kəhrpa frašusaṯ[5a]   in the shape of a bird.

auuaēnō[5b] *x*ⁿ*arənō fraēštō*[6]   Not seeing the Glory shining Yima

   yō yimō xšaētō huuąθβō   of good herds was driven off.

brāsaṯ[7] *yimō ašātō*[7a]   Unhappy Yima started to wander about

dəuš.manahiiāica[8] *hō stərətō*[9]   and being laid low because of his evil–
    mindedness he kept himself hidden on

   nidāraṯ[10] *upairi ząm*[10a]   the earth.'

35. *paoirīm*[1a] *x*ⁿ*arənō apanəmata*[1b]   'For the first time the Glory went away;

   *x*ⁿ*arənō yimaṯ*[1] *haca xšaētāṯ*[2]   the Glory, from shining Yima.

šusaṯ[2a] *x*ⁿ*arənō yimaṯ*[2b] *haca*   The Glory hastened away from Yima,

   vīuuaŋhušāṯ[2c]   the son of Vivasvant,

mərəγahe[3] *kəhrpa vārəγnahe*[4]   in the shape of a bird of prey.

*aom x*ⁿ*arənō haŋgəuruuaiiata*[4a]   That one, the Glory, Miθra seized,

   miθrō yō[4b] *vouru.gaoiiaoitiš*[4c]   (Miθra) of wide pastures,

---

[4] There is an error of logic. It should be: 'before his lying'.

yō srut̰.gaošō[4d] *hazaŋra.yaoxštiš*[4e]	whose ears hearken and who has a
miϑrəm[4f] *vīspanąm*[4g] *dax́iiunąm*	thousand skills. We worship Miϑra
daŋhupaitim yazamaide	the Lord of all lands,
yim fradaϑat̰ ahurō[4h] *mazdå̄*	whom Ahura Mazdā created
x^varənan^vhastəməm	as the most endowed with Glory
mańiiauuanąm yazatanąm	among the spiritual adorable ones.'

36. *yat̰ bitīm*[1a] *x^varənō apanəmata*[1b]   'When the Glory went away for the sec-
  x^varənō yimat̰[1c] *haca xšaētāt̰*   ond time, the Glory from shining Yima,
  śusat̰[1d] *x^varənō yimat̰ haca*   the Glory hastened away from Yima,
    vīuuaŋhušāt̰[1e]   the son of Vivasvant,
  mərəγahe[1f] *kəhrpa vārəγnahe*[1g]   in the shape of a bird of prey.
  aom x^varənō haŋgəuruuaiiata[1]   That one, the Glory, Θraētaona seized,
  vīsō[1h] *puϑrō å̄ϑβiiānōiš*[1i]   (Θraētaona,) the son of the Āϑβiia-
    [1k]*vīsō sūraiiå̄*[1l] *ϑraētaonō*   clan, of the heroic family,
  yat̰[1m] *ās mašiiānąm*[1n] *vərəϑrauuanąm*[1o]   so that he was among victorious men
    vərəϑrauuastəmō[1p] *ańiiō*[2]   the most victorious, apart from
    zaraϑuštrāt̰   Zaraϑuštra.'

37. *yō janat̰ ažim*[1a] *dahākəm* [(= Y 9,8)   'Who slew the Dragon Dahāka,
  ϑrizafanəm[4] *ϑrikamərəδəm*[5]   who had three mouths, three heads,
  xšuuaš.ašīm[6] *hazaŋrā.yaoxštim*[7]   six eyes, a thousand skills,
  aš.aojaŋhəm[8] *daēuuīm*[9] +*drujim*[10]   the very mighty, devilish Falsehood,
  aγəm gaēϑåuuiiō[11] *druuantəm*[12]   evil for the world, the deceitful one,
  yąm aš.aojastəmąm +*drujim*[13]   whom the Evil Spirit brought forth
  fraca kərəntat̰ aŋrō[14] *mańiiuš*[15]   as the mightiest Falsehood
  aoi[16] *yąm astuuaitīm gaēϑąm*[17]]   against the corporeal world, for the
  mahrkāi ašahe gaēϑanąm   destruction of the world of Truth.'

38. *yat̰*[1a] *ϑritīm*[1b] *x^varənō apanəmata*   'When the Glory went away for the
  x^varənō yimat̰[1c] *haca xšaētāt̰*[1d]   third time, the Glory from shining
  śusat̰[1e] *x^varənō yimat̰ haca vīuuaŋhušāt̰*[1f]   Yima, the Glory hastened away from
  mərəγahe kəhrpa vārəγnahe[1g]   Yima, the son of Vivasvant, in the
  aom x^varənō haŋgəuruuaiiata[1h]   shape of a bird of prey.
  naire.manå̄[1] *kərəsāspō*[1i]   That one, the Glory,
                                                        manly-minded Kərəsāspa seized

yaṱ ās[1k] mašiiānąm[1l] uγranąm[1m]
aojištō[1n] ańiiō zaraϑuštrāṱ[1o]
nairiiaiiāṱ[2] parō[2a] ×hąm.varətōiṱ[3]

so that he was among strong men
the mightiest, apart from Zaraϑuštra,
on account of his manly defence.'

39. yaṱ[1a] dim upaŋhacaṱ[1b]
 yā[1c] uγra[1d] naire[1e] hąm.varəitiš[1]
[1f]nairiiąm hąm.varəitim[2] yazamaide
ərəδβō.zəṇgąm[3] ax^vafniiąm[3a]
āsitō.gātum[3b] jaγāurum[4]
yā upaŋhacaṱ kərəsāspəm[4a]

'Since the mighty, manly defence
accompanied him.
We worship the manly defence, which
is always on its feet, without sleep,
which is awake even when lying on the
bed, which accompanied Kərəsāspa.'

40. yō janaṱ[1a] ažim sruuarəm[1b]
yim aspō.garəm nərə.garəm[1]
yim višauuaṇtəm[1c] zairitəm
yim upairi viš[2] +araoδaṱ[2]
xšuuaēpaiia[3] +vanaiia.barəšna[4]
yim upairi viš +araoδaṱ
ārštiiō.barəza zairitəm[5]
yim upairi kərəsāspō
aiiaŋha pitum pacata
ā rapiϑβinəm zruuānəm
tafsaṱca[6] hō mairiiō [(= Y 9,11)
        x^īsaṱca[18]
frąš aiiaŋhō[19] frasparaṱ[20]
yaēšiiaṇtīm[21] āpəm +parāńhāṱ[22]
parąš[23] tarštō[24] apatacaṱ[25]]
naire.manå kərəsāspō

'Who slew the horned Dragon,
the horse-devouring, man-devouring,
poisonous, yellow one.
On whom the poisonous plant grew
at the tail as high as a tree.
On whom the poisonous plant grew
as high as a spear, on the yellow one.
On whom Kərəsāspa
cooked his meal in an iron pot
around midday.
The villain became hot
and started sweating;
forwards he kicked against the pot,
he wanted to upset the boiling water.
Frightened manly-minded
Kərəsāspa jumped aside.'

41. yō janaṱ
gaṇdarəβəm[1] yim zairi.pāšnəm
yō apataṱ vīzafārō[2]
mərəxšānō[2a] gaēϑå å astuuaitīš ašahe
yō janaṱ[2b]
hunauuō yaṱ paϑanaiia[3] nauua[4]
hunauuasca[4a] niuuikahe[5]
hunauuasca[5a] dāštaiiānōiš[5b]

'Who slew
Gaṇdarəβa, who had a yellow heel, who
rushed about with wide-open mouth
to destroy the world of Truth;
who slew
the nine sons of Paϑana,
the sons of Niuuika,
the sons of Dāštaiiāni;

yō janaṯ[5c]

   zaraṇiiō.pusəm[6] *hitāspəm*[7]

   varəšaomca dānaiianəm

   pitaonəmca[8] *aš.pairikəm*[9]

who slew
Hitāspa of golden diadem, and Varə-
šauua, the son of Dāna, and Pitaona
accompanied by powerful witches.'

42. *yō janaṯ*[1a] *arəzō.šamanəm*[1]

   nairiiąm.hąm.[×]*varəitiuuaṇtəm*[2]

  taxməm frāzuštəm . . . uštəm[3]

  jirəm[4] *zbarəmnəm*[4a] *jiγāurum*[5]

  afrakatacim[6] [+]*barō.zušəm*[7]

  apa.disəm[8] [+]*aṅiiāi dāuru*[9]

  apastanaṇhō[9a] *gatō.arəzahe*[10.11]

'Who slew Arəzō.šamana
skilled in manly defence,
the brave, popular, desired one, the
lively, moving around, vigilant one,
running in the first battle–line, rejoicing in booty, turning away the spear
to another one, (the spear) of someone
. . . whose battle has been joined (?).'

43. *yō janaṯ*[1a] *snāuuiδkəm*[1]

   yim sruuō.zanəm[2] *asəṇgō.gāum*[3]

 hō auuaϑa viiāxmaṅiiata

  apərənāiiu[4] *ahmi nōiṯ pərənāiiu*[4a]

  yezi bauuāni[4b] *pərənāiiu*[4a]

  ząm caxrəm kərənauuāne

  asmanəm raϑəm kərənauuāne

'Who slew Snāuuiδka who
had leaden jaws and hands of stone.
He boasted in the following way:
"I am a minor, not yet of full age.
When I come of age
I will make the earth into my wheel,
I will make the sky into my chariot!" '

44. *auuanaiieni spəṇtəm maṅiium*

   haca raoxšna[1] *garō nmāna*[1]

 uspataiieni[2] *aṇrəm maṅiium*

  ərəγata haca [×]*daožaṇᵛha*[2a]

 tē mē vāšəm[2b] *ϑaṇjaiiåṇte*[3]

  spəṇtasca maṅiiuš aṇrasca

 yezi mąm nōiṯ janāṯ

  naire.manå[4] *kərəsāspō*[5]

 təm [×]*janaṯ naire.manå*[4] *kərəsāspō*[5]

  auua apanəm gaiiehe

  ⟨*fra*⟩*sānəm*[6] *uštānahe*[7]

ahe raiia . . . (= Yt 19.13) . . .

. . . *tåscā yazamaide*

' "I will fetch down the Bounteous Spirit
from the radiant House of Welcome,
I will raise up the Evil Spirit
from the tumultuous Hell.
Both shall pull my chariot,
the Bounteous and the Evil Spirit —
provided that manly–minded Kərəsāspa
does not kill me."
Manly–minded Kərəsāspa struck him
down for the end of his life,
for the destruction of his vitality.
On account of his splendour . . .
and these (female Entities) we worship.'

Karde VII

45. *uɣrəm[1b] ax^varətəm[1] x^varənō*
   mazdaδātəm yazamaide
   aš.vaṇdrəm[2] uparō.kairīm[2a]
   ϑamnaŋ^vhaṇtəm[3] varəcaŋ^vhaṇtəm[3]
     yaoxštiuuaṇtəm[3a]
   taraδātəm[3b] aṅiiāiš dāmąn

'We worship the mighty gleaming Glory
created by Mazdā,
the highly praised, supreme worker,
determined, energetic,
   skilful,
overcoming the other creatures.'

46. *yahmi paiti ×parətaēϑe[1]*
   spəṇtasca maṅiiuš aŋrasca
   aētahmi paiti at[2] ax^varəte[3]
   aδāt ×aštō[4] fraŋharəcaiiat
   ×āsištō[5] katarascit
   spəṇtō maṅiiuš[5a] aštəm[6] fraŋharəcaiiat
   [7]vohuca manō aṣ̌əmca vahištəm
   ātrəmca[8] ahurahe mazdā̊ puϑrəm
   aŋrō maṅiiuš[5a] aštəm[8a] fraŋharəcaiiat[7]
   akəmca manō aēšəməmca[8b]
     xruui.drum[9]
   ažimca[9a] dahākəm
   spitiiurəmca[10] yimō.kərəṇtəm

'For which the Bounteous and the Evil
Spirit struggled against each other,
for this one, which is gleaming.
Then each one sent forth
his swiftest messengers: The Bounteous Spirit sent forth as his messenger
Good Thinking and Best Truth
and the Fire, the son of Ahura Mazdā.
The Evil Spirit sent forth as his messenger Bad Thinking and Rage,
   whose attack is cruel,
and the Dragon Dahāka,
and Spitiiura who cut Yima to pieces.'

47. *aδāt ×fraša[1a] hąm.rāzaiiata[1]*
   ātarš[1b] mazdā̊ ahurahe
   uiti auuaϑa maŋhānō[2]
   aētat x^varənō haṇgərəfšāne[3]
   yat ax^varətəm[4]
   āat hē[4a] paskāt fraduuarat
   ažiš ϑrizafā̊ duždaēnō
   ×uiti[4a] zaxšaϑrəm[5] daomnō

'Then the Fire of Ahura Mazdā
stepped forward (to the contest)
thinking thus:
"I want to grab this Glory
which is gleaming!"
Then the three–mouthed, evil–minded
Dragon ran forward from behind him
uttering words of abuse thus:'

48. *iṇja[1] auuat haṇdaēsaiiaŋ^vha[2]*
   ātarš[2a] mazdā̊ ahurahe
   yezi aētat niiāsā̊ŋhe
   yat ax^varətəm

' "*Inja!* Bear that in mind,
Fire of Ahura Mazdā:
If you seize this
gleaming one,

frā ϑβ̨am paiti apāϑa	I will fall upon you!
nōiṯ apaiia uzraocaiiāi	Thereafter you will not blaze up
z̨am paiti ahuraδātam[2b]	upon the Earth created by Ahura
ϑrāϑrāi ašahe gaēϑan̨am	to protect the world of Truth!"
aδa[3] *ātarš zasta paiti*	Thereupon the Fire withdrew
apa.gǝuruuaiiaṯ[4]	his two hands
fraxšni[5] *uštānō.cinahiia*[6]	because of prudent love of his own life,
yaϑa ažiš[7] *+biβiuuā̊ +ā̊ŋha*[7]	as the Dragon was terrifying.'

49. *aδāṯ*[1] *frašá ham̨.duuaraṯ*[2]   'Then the three–mouthed, evil–minded
      ažiš ϑrizafā̊[3] *duždaēnō*[3a]   Dragon ran forward (to the contest)
      uiti auuaϑa maŋhānō[4]   thus thinking:
      aētaṯ x^varǝnō haṉgrǝfšāne[5]   "I want to grab this
      yaṯ ax^varǝtǝm   gleaming Glory!"
      āaṯ hē paskāṯ ham̨.rāzaiiata[5a]   Then the Fire of Ahura Mazdā stepped
      ātarš mazdā̊ ahurahe   (to the contest) from behind him
      uiti vacǝbiš[6] *aojanō*   uttering words thus:'

50. *tiṉja*[1] *auuaṯ haṉdaēsaiiaŋ^vha*[2]   ' "*Tinja*! Bear that in mind,
      aže[3] *ϑrizafǝm dahāka*   three–mouthed Dragon Dahāka:
      yezi aētaṯ niiāsā̊ŋhe   If you seize this
      yaṯ ax^varǝtǝm   gleaming one,
      frā ϑβ̨am zadaŋha[4] *paiti uzuxšāne*   I will flare up at your buttocks.
      zafarǝ[5] *paiti uzraocaiieni*   I will blaze up at your mouth.
      nōiṯ apaiia afrapatāi[6]   Thereafter you will not walk about
      z̨am paiti ahuraδātam   upon the Earth created by Ahura
      mahrkāi ašahe gaēϑan̨am   to destroy the world of Truth!"
      aδa[7] *ažiš gauua paiti*   Thereupon the Dragon withdrew
      apa.gǝuruuaiiaṯ   his two hands
      fraxšni[8] *uštānō.cinahiia*[8a]   because of prudent love of his own life,
      yaϑa[8b] *ātarš*[8c] *+biβiuuā̊ +ā̊ŋha*[9] as the Fire was terrifying.'

51. *aētaṯ*[1] *x^varǝnō frapinuuata*[2]   'This Glory surged forward
      auui[3] *zraiiō vouru.kašǝm*   to Lake Vourukaša.
      ā.dim haϑra haṉgǝuruuaiiaṯ[3a]   At once seized it
      apam̨ napā̊ auruuaṯ.aspō   Apam̨ Napāt, owner of swift horses,

tatca⁴ iziieiti⁵

   apąm napā̊ auruuaṯ.aspō

aētaṯ xᵛarənō haṇgrəfšāne

   yaṯ axᵛarətəm

   × bune⁵ᵃ zraiiaŋhō gufrahe

   bune jafranąm vairiianąm

desires it

Apąm Napāt, owner of swift horses:

"I want to grab this

gleaming Glory,

at the bottom of the unfathomable lake,

at the bottom of the deep bays." '

52. bərəzaṇtəm¹ᵃ ahurəm xšaϑrīm¹

   xšaētəm apąm napātəm

   auruuaṯ.aspəm yazamaide

aršānəm zauuanō.sūm²

   yō × nərə̄š ²ᵃ daδa

   yō × nərə̄š ²ᵃ tatāša³

   yō upāpō yazatō

   sruṯ.gaošōtəmō³ᵃ asti yezimnō⁴

'We worship the high, ruling Lord,

shining Apąm Napāt,

owner of swift horses.

The male, who prospers through liba-

tions, who created the men,

who fashioned the men, the adorable

one who lives in the waters, whose ears

hear best when he is being worshipped.'

53. āaṯ¹ vō kasciṯ mašiiānąm¹ᵃ

   uiti mraoṯ ahurō mazdā̊

   āi ašāum zaraϑuštra

xᵛarənō axᵛarətəm¹ᵇ isaēta²

   + aϑ a³ +urunō³ hō⁴ rātanąm

   raoxšni.xšnutəm⁵ išā̊ŋhaēta⁶

   + aϑ a⁶ᵃ +urunō ⁶ᵃ hō rātanąm

   pouru.xšnutəm⁸ išā̊ŋhaēta⁸ᵃ

   + aϑ a⁹ +urunō ⁹ hō¹⁰ rātanąm¹¹

' "Whoever of you mortals,"

— thus spake Ahura Mazdā,

o truthful Zaraϑuštra, —

"desires for himself the gleaming Glory,

in this way he may seek to gain radiant

strengthening among the gifts for the

soul. In this way he may seek to gain

much strengthening among the gifts for

the soul. In this way he may seek to

gain among the gifts for the soul ..." '

54. təm¹ hacāṯ ašiš

   pouruš.xᵛā̊ϑra² spāra.dāšta³

   sūra gə̄ušca vāstraheca

təm hacāṯ vərəϑrəm vīspō.aiiārəm⁴

   amaēniᵞnəm tarō.yārəm⁵

āaṯ ana vərəϑra hacimnō⁵ᵃ

   vanāṯ × haēnå̄ × yå̄⁵ᵇ xruuišiieitīš⁶

āaṯ ana vərəϑra hacimnō⁵ᵃ

   vanāṯ × vīspə +ṯbišaiiaṇtō⁷

' "Reward will accompany him, grant-

ing much well–being, granting prosper-

ity, ruling over cattle and pasture.

Victory will accompany him all days,

defeat (of enemies) in (their) attack

(will accompany him) over the years.

Accompanied by this victory he will

defeat blood–thirsty hostile armies.

Accompanied by this victory

he will defeat all foes."

ahe raiia x^varənaŋhaca	On account of his splendour and glory
təm yazāi surunuuata yasna	I will worship him with audible vener-
uγrəm ax^varətəm x^varənō	ation, the mighty, gleaming Glory, cre-
mazdaδātəm zaoϑrābiiō	ated by Mazdā (I will worship) with
uγrəm ax^varətəm x^varənō	libations. We worship the mighty,
mazdaδātəm yazamaide	gleaming Glory created by Mazdā
+haoma +yō⁷ᵃ gauua ...(= Yt 19.13)	with Haoma mixed with milk ...
... *tā̊scā yazamaide*	and these (female Entities) we worship.'

Karde VIII

55. *uγrəm ax^varətəm¹* [(= Yt 19.45)   'We worship the mighty gleaming
     x^varənō   Glory
    mazdaδātəm yazamaide   created by Mazdā,
    aš.vaṇdrəm² uparō.kairīm   the highly praised, supreme worker,
    ϑamnaŋ^vhaṇtəm³ varəcaŋ^vhaṇtəm³ determined, energetic,
     yaoxštiuuaṇtəm   skilful,
    taraδātəm] *ańiiāiš dāmąn*   overcoming the other creatures.'

56. *yaṯ isaṯ¹ mairiiō tuiriiō¹ᵇ fraŋrase²*   '(The Glory,) which the Turanian vil-
    zraiiaŋhō³ vouru.kašahe³ᵃ   lain Fraŋrasiian desired out of Lake
  maγnō apa.spaiiaṯ⁴ vastrā̊   Vourukaša. (He was) naked, he had
    taṯ x^varənō isō yaṯ asti   thrown aside his garments desiring this
    airiianąm dax́iiunąm   Glory which belongs to the Aryan
    zātanąm⁵ azātanąmca   lands, the born and unborn, and which
    yaṯca ašaonō zaraϑuštrahe   belongs to truthful Zaraϑuštra.
  ā taṯ⁶ x^varənō frazgaδata   He dashed forward to the Glory,
  ⁷*taṯ x^varənō apatacaṯ⁷*   the Glory rushed away,
    taṯ x^varənō apa.hiδaṯ⁸   the Glory escaped.
  aδa⁸ᵃ hāu⁹ apaγžārō buuaṯ¹⁰   Thereupon emerged that inlet
    zraiiaŋhō vouru.kašahe   of Lake Vourukaša,
    vairiš yō haosrauuå̊¹¹ nąma   the bay called "Well–Famed".'

57. *āaṯ us.pataṯ fraŋrase turō¹ᵃ*   'Then Fraŋrasiian the very strong
    aš.varəcā̊   Turanian,
  spitama zaraϑuštra   o Spitāma Zaraϑuštra,

zraiiaŋhaṯ haca vouru.kašāṯ
aγąm daoiϑrīm¹ daomnō
⁺iϑa² iϑa³ yaϑna⁴ ahmāi
nōiṯ taṯ xᵛarənō pairi.abaom
yaṯ asti airiianąm dax́iiunąm
zātanąm azātanąmca
yaṯca⁵ ašaonō zaraϑuštrahe

came out of Lake Vourukaša
speaking evil words of abuse:
"iϑa iϑa yaϑna ahmāi!
I have not been able to get hold of that
Glory which belongs to the Aryan
lands, the born and unborn and which
belongs to truthful Zaraϑuštra!" '

58. ˣuuaēm¹ hąm.raēϑβaiieni
vīspa taršuca² xšuδraca³
masanaca vaŋhanaca sraiianaca
⁺ϑβązjaiti⁴ ahurō mazdā̊
paitišå̄⁵ dāmąn daϑāno
āaṯ auua.pataṯ fraŋrase turō⁵ᵃ aš.varəcā̊
spitama zaraϑuštra
auui zraiiō vouru.kašəm

' "I will mix up everything,
both solid and liquid, because of
its greatness, goodness and beauty.
Ahura Mazdā becomes oppressed
when creating the hostile creatures."
And Fraŋrasiian the very strong Tura-
nian, o Spitāma Zaraϑuštra,
went down to Lake Vourukaša.'

59. āṯbitīm¹ maγnō apa.spaiiaṯ vastrā̊
taṯ xᵛarənō isō yaṯ asti
airiianąm dax́iiunąm²
[(= Yt 19.56) zātanąm⁵ azātanąmca
yaṯca⁶ ašaonō zaraϑuštrahe
ā taṯ⁶ xᵛarənō frazgaδata
⁷taṯ xᵛarənō apatacaṯ⁷
taṯ xᵛarənō apa.hiδaṯ⁸
aδaδ⁸ᵃ hāu⁹ apaγžārō buuaṯ¹⁰]
zraiiaŋhō vouru.kašahe
vairiš yō ˣvaŋhazdā̊³ nąma

'For the second time (he was) naked, he
had thrown aside his garments desiring
that Glory which belongs to the Aryan
lands, the born and unborn, and which
belongs to truthful Zaraϑuštra.
He dashed forward to the Glory,
the Glory rushed away,
the Glory escaped.
Thereupon emerged that inlet
of Lake Vourukaša, the bay
called "Giver of the Very Good".'

60. āaṯ us.pataṯ fraŋrase turō¹ᵃ
aš.varəcō
spitama zaraϑuštra
zraiiaŋhaṯ haca vouru.kašāṯ
aγąm daoiϑrīm daomnō
ˣiϑa¹ iϑa² yaϑna³ ahmāi⁴
⁺auuaϑa⁵ iϑa⁶ yaϑna⁷ kahmāi

'Then Fraŋrasiian the very strong
Turanian,
o Spitāma Zaraϑuštra,
came out of Lake Vourukaša
speaking evil words of abuse:
"iϑa iϑa yaϑna ahmāi
auuaϑa iϑa yaϑna kahmāi!

nōiṯ taṯ xᵛarənō pairi.abaom   I have not been able to get hold of that
    yaṯ asti airiianąm dax́iiunąm   Glory which belongs to the Aryan
    [(= Yt 19.57) zātanąm azātanąmca   lands, the born and unborn and which
    yaṯca⁵ ašaonō zaraϑuštrahe]   belongs to truthful Zaraϑuštra!" '

61. [(= Yt 19.58) ˣuuaēm¹   ' "I will mix up
    hąm.raēϑβaiieni   everything,
    vīspa taršuca² xšuδraca³   both solid and liquid, because of
    masanaca vaŋhanaca sraiianaca   its greatness, goodness and beauty.
   ⁺ϑβ a̦zjaiti⁴ ahurō mazdā̊   Ahura Mazdā becomes oppressed
    paitišā̊⁵ dāmąn daϑānō   when creating the hostile creatures."
   āaṯ auua.pataṯ fraŋrase tūrō aš.varəcā̊   And Fraŋrasiian the very strong Tura-
    spitama zaraϑuštra]   nian, o Spitāma Zaraϑuštra,
    auui zraiiō vouru.kašəm   went down to Lake Vourukaša.'

62. āϑritīm apa.spaiiaṯ vastrā̊   'For the third time he had thrown aside
    taṯ xᵛarənō isō yaṯ asti   his garments desiring that Glory
    airiianąm dax́iiunąm   which belongs to the Aryan lands,
    [(= Yt 19.56) zātanąm⁵ azātanąmca   the born and unborn, and which
    yaṯca ašaonō zaraϑuštrahe   belongs to truthful Zaraϑuštra.
   ā taṯ⁶ xᵛarənō frazgaδata   He dashed forward to the Glory,
   ⁷taṯ xᵛarənō apatacaṯ⁷   the Glory rushed away,
    taṯ xᵛarənō apa.hiδaṯ⁸   the Glory escaped.
   aδa⁸ᵃ hāu⁹ apaγžārō buuaṯ¹⁰]   Thereupon emerged an inlet
    zraiiaŋhō vouru.kašahe   of Lake Vourukaša, a stream
    āfš yā aβžḍānuua¹ nąma   of water called "Water-stream".'

63. āaṯ us.pataṯ fraŋrase turō¹ᵃ   'Then Fraŋrasiian the very strong
    aš.varəcā̊   Turanian,
    spitama zaraϑuštra   o Spitāma Zaraϑuštra,
    zraiiaŋhaṯ haca vouru.kašāṯ   came out of Lake Vourukaša
    aγąm daoiϑrīm daomnō   speaking evil words of abuse:
   ⁺iϑa¹ iϑa² yaϑna³ ahmāi   "iϑa iϑa yaϑna ahmāi
   ˣauuaϑa⁴ iϑa yaϑna³ ahmāi   auuaϑa iϑa yaϑna ahmāi
   ⁵āuuōiia iϑa yaϑna⁵ ahmāi   āuuōiia iϑa yaϑna ahmāi!
   nōiṯ taṯ xᵛarənō pairi.abaom   I have not been able to get hold of that

yat̰ asti airiianąm dax̌iiunąm	Glory which belongs to the Aryan
zātanąm azātanąmca	lands, the born and unborn, and which
yat̰ca ašaonō zaraϑuštrahe	belongs to truthful Zaraϑuštra!" '

64. *nōit̰ tat̰ xᵛarənō pairi.abauuat̰* — 'He did not get hold of that Glory
   yat̰ asti airiianąm dax̌iiunąm — which belongs to the Aryan lands,
   zātanąm azātanąmca — the born and unborn, and which
   yat̰ca ašaonō zaraϑuštrahe — belongs to truthful Zaraϑuštra.

ahe raiia [(= Yt 19.54) *xᵛarənaŋhaca* — On account of his splendour and glory
   təm yazāi surunuuata yasna — I will worship him with audible venera-
uγrəm axᵛarətəm xᵛarənō — tion, the mighty gleaming Glory created
   mazdaδātəm zaoϑrābiiō — by Mazdā (I will worship) with liba-
uγrəm axᵛarətəm xᵛarənō — tions. We worship the mighty gleaming
   mazdaδātəm yazamaide — Glory created by Mazdā
⁺*haoma* ⁺*yō⁷ᵃ gauua* ... (= Yt 19.13) — with Haoma mixed with milk ...
   ...] *tā̊scā yazamaide* — and these (female Entities) we worship.'

Karde IX

65. *uγrəm axᵛarətəm¹* [(= Yt 19.45) — 'We worship the mighty gleaming
      xᵛarənō — Glory
   mazdaδātəm yazamaide — created by Mazdā,
   aš.vandrəm² uparō.kairīm — the highly praised, supreme worker,
   ϑamnaŋᵛhantəm³ varəcaŋᵛhantəm³ — determined, energetic,
      yaoxštiuuantəm — skilful,
   taraδātəm] *ańiiāiš dāmąn* — overcoming the other creatures.'

66. *yat̰ upaŋhacaiti¹* — 'Which accompanies (the one) who
   yō auuaδāt̰ fraxšaiieite² — rules from that place, where the Lake
yaϑa zraiiō yat̰ kąsaēm³ haētumatəm⁴ — Kąsaoiia (is), where Haētumaṇt (is),
yaϑa gairiš yō ⁺*usaδā̊⁵* — where Mount Usaδā (is), around which
   yim aißitō⁶ paoirīš⁶ᵃ āpō — from all sides the many streams follow-
   hąm gairišācō⁷ jasəṇtō⁸ — ing along the slope come together.'

67. *auui təm auui.haṇtacaiti* [1]   'Into this (lake) comes together,
auui [2] *təm auui.hąm.vazaite* [3]   into this (lake) flows
  x^vāstraca [4] *huuaspaca fradaϑa*   X^vāstrā and Huuaspā and Fradaϑā,
  x^varənaŋ^vhaitica [5] *yā srīra* [6]   and beautiful X^varənaŋ^vhaitī,
  uštauuaitica [7] *yā sūra*   and strong Uštauuaitī,
  uruuaδca [8] *pouru.vāstra*   and Uruuā, rich in pastures,
  ərəzica [9] *zarənumatica* [10]   and ∃rəzī and Zarənumatī.
auui təm auui.haṇtacaiti   Into this (lake) comes together,
auui təm [11] *auui.hąm.vazaite* [2]   into this (lake) flows
  ×*haē⟨tumā̊⟩* [12] *raēuuā̊ x^varənaŋ^vhā̊* [13]   Haētumant, the opulent and splendid
  spaētinīš [14] *varəmīš* ×*sispəmnō* [15]   one, swelling with white waves,
  ×*niiaŋhəmnō* [16] *paoirīš* [17] *vōiγnā̊*   causing many floods.'

68. *hacaiti dim aspahe aojō*   'Strength of a horse accompanies him,
[1]*hacaiti uštrahe aojō* [1]   strength of a camel accompanies (him),
  hacaiti vīrahe aojō   strength of a hero accompanies (him),
  hacaiti kauuaēm x^varənō   the Glory of the Kauui–dynasty accom-
[1]*astica ahmi ašāum zaraϑuštra*   panies him. In this (= Haētumaṇt), o
  auuauuat̰ kauuaēm x^varənō [1]   truthful Zaraϑuštra, is so much Glory
  yaϑa yat̰ iδa anairiiā̊ daŋhūš [2]   of the Kauui–dynasty, that it could
  hakat̰ usca us.frāuuaiiōit̰ [3]   completely sweep aside all non–Aryan
                                                    inhabitants from there at once.'

69. *aϑra* [1] *pascaēta vaozirəm* [2]   'There then they may come along
  baoδaṇtō šuδəm [2a] *taršnəmca* [2b]   feeling hunger and thirst,
  baoδaṇtō aotəm uruuāxrəmca [3]   feeling cold and heat.
tat̰ asti kauuaēm x^varənō   This is the Glory of the Kauui–dynasty,
  ϑrāϑrəm airiianąm daxiiunąm   the protection of the Aryan lands,
  gə̄ušca paṇcō.hiiaiiāi [4]   of the cow of five species,
  auuaŋhe narąm ašaonąm   to help the truthful men
  daēnaiiā̊sca māzdaiiasnōiš   and the Mazdayasnian religion.
ahe raiia ... (= Yt 19.54) ...   On account of his splendour ...
... *tā̊scā yazamaide*   and these (female Entities) we worship.'

Karde X

70. *uγrəm kauuaēm* [(= Yt 19.9)
    x^varənō

    'We worship the mighty Glory of the Kauui–dynasty

    mazdaδātəm yazamaide

    created by Mazdā,

    aš.vandrəm[1] *uparō.kairīm*

    the highly praised, supreme worker,

    ϑamnaŋ^vhantəm[2] *varəcaŋ^vhantəm*[3]
    yaoxštiuuantəm

    determined, energetic, skilful,

    taraδātəm[4]] *ańiiāiš dāmąn*

    overcoming the other creatures.'

71. *yaṯ upaŋhacaṯ kauuaēm kauuātəm*[1]

    'Which accompanied Kauui Kauuāta,

    yimca kauuaēm aipi.vohum[2]

    and Kauui Aipi.vohu,

    [2a]*yimca kauuaēm usaδanəm*[2a]

    and Kauui Usaδan,

    [3]*yimca kauuaēm aršnəm*[3]

    and Kauui Aršan,

    yimca kauuaēm pisinəm[4]

    and Kauui Pisina,

    yimca kauuaēm biiaršānəm

    and Kauui Biiaršan,

    [4a]*yimca kauuaēm siiāuuaršānəm*[4a]

    and Kauui Siiāuuaršan.'

72. *yaṯ*[1] *bāun*[2]

    'So that they became

    vīspe auruua vīspe taxma

    all swift, all brave,

    vīspe ϑamnaŋhunta[3]

    all determined,

    vīspe varəcaŋhunta[4]

    all energetic,

    vīspe yaoxštiuuanta

    all skilful,

    vīspe ×*darši.kaire*[5] +*kauuae*[6]

    all audaciously acting Kauuis.

    ahe raiia ... (= Yt 19.13) ...

    On account of his splendour ...

    ... *tā̊scā yazamaide*

    and these (female Entities) we worship.'

Karde XI

73. *uγrəm kauuaēm* [(= Yt 19.9)
    x^varənō

    'We worship the mighty Glory of the Kauui–dynasty

    mazdaδātəm yazamaide

    created by Mazdā,

    aš.vandrəm[1] *uparō.kairīm*

    the highly praised, supreme worker,

    ϑamnaŋ^vhantəm[2] *varəcaŋ^vhantəm*[3]
    yaoxštiuuantəm

    determined, energetic, skilful,

    taraδātəm[4]] *ańiiāiš dāmąn*

    overcoming the other creatures.'

74. *yat̰ upaŋhacat̰ kauuaēm*
       haosrauuaŋhəm[1]   'Which accompanied Kauui
                                                       Haosrauuah,
amaheca paiti hutāštahe   for his well-created impetuosity,
   vərəϑraɣnaheca [(= Yt 13.133) *paiti*   for his victoriousness
       ahuraδātahe   created by Ahura,
   vanaiṇtiiā̊sca paiti uparatātō   for his conquering superiority,
   saŋᵛhasca[2] *paiti husastaiiā̊*[3]   for his well–ordered order,
   saŋᵛhasca[2] *paiti amuiiamnaiiā̊*[4]   for his unwavering order,
   saŋᵛhasca paiti auuanəmnaiiā̊   for his invincible order,
   haϑrauuataheca paiti   and for the immediate victory
       hamərəϑanąm[5]]   over enemies;'

75. [(= Yt 13.134) *druuaheca paiti*   'and for his robust
       aojaŋhō   strength,
   xᵛarənaŋhasca paiti mazdaδātahe   and for his Glory created by Mazdā,
   tanuiiā̊sca[1] *paiti druuatātō*   and for the health of his body,
   āsnaiiā̊sca paiti vaŋhuiiā̊ frazaṇtōiš[2]   and for noble, good offspring,
   daŋraiiā̊ viiāxanaiiā̊   which is knowledgeable, eloquent,
   xšōiϑniiō[3] *spitidōiϑraiiā̊*   shining, with bright eyes,
   ązō.būjō huuīraiiā̊   rescuing from trouble (and) manly,
   huzaṇtə̄uš paiti aparaiiā̊   for the future, undisputed
   viiarəϑiiaiiā̊[4] *vahištahe aŋhə̄uš*]   recognition of the best life;'

76. [(= Yt 13.135) *xšaϑraheca paiti*   'and for his splendid
       bānumatō   rule,
   darəɣaiiā̊sca paiti darəɣō.jītōiš   and for his long–lasting lifetime,
   vīspanąmca paiti aiiaptanąm[1]]   and for all boons,
   vīspanąmca[1a] *paiti baēšazanąm*   and for all cures.'

77. *yat̰* [+]*paiti*[1]   'So that Kauui Haosrauuah
   kauua haosrauua[1a] [×]*təm*[1b] *kərəsəm*[2] came close to that robber
   upa tąm[3] *carətąm*[4] *yąm darəɣąm*   on that long racecourse
   nauua.frāϑβərəsąm[5] *razurəm*   through the forest of nine glades.
   yat̰ dim mairiiō nurəm [+]*manō*[5a]   When the agile–minded villain fought
   aspaēšu paiti parətata[6]   him in the chariot race,
   vīspe[6a] *bauuaṯ aiβi.vańiiā̊*   Kauui Haosrauuah, the lord,

ahurō kauua haosrauua[6b]	was victorious in all respects
mairīm[6c] *tuirīm*[6d] *fraŋrasiiānəm*[6e]	over the Turanian villain Fraŋrasiian.
baṇdaiiaṯ[6f] *×kərəsauuazdaŋhəm*[7]	He (= Haosrauuah) bound Kərəsauuazdah,
puϑrō[8] *kaēna*[9] *siiāuuaršānāi*[10]	(he,) the avenging son of Siiāuuaršan,
zurō.jatahe[10a] *narahe*[11]	the treacherously killed man,
aγraēraϑahe narauuahe[12]	(and as the avenger) of Aγraēraϑa,
	the offspring of Naru.
ahe raiia ... (= Yt 19.13) ...	On account of his splendour ...
... *tåscā yazamaide*	and these (female Entities) we worship.'

Karde XII

78. *uγrəm kauuaēm* [(= Yt 19.9) *xᵛarənō*	'We worship the mighty Glory of the Kauui–dynasty
mazdaδātəm yazamaide	created by Mazdā,
aš.vaṇdrəm[1] *uparō.kairīm*	the highly praised, supreme worker,
ϑamnaŋᵛhaṇtəm[2] *varəcaŋᵛhaṇtəm*[3]	determined, energetic,
yaoxštiuuaṇtəm	skilful,
taraδātəm[4]] *aṅiiāiš dāmąn*	overcoming the other creatures.'

79. *yaṯ upaŋhacaṯ ašauuanəm zaraϑuštrəm*	'Which accompanied truthful Zaraϑuštra
anumatōe daēnaiiāi[1]	to think according to the Religion,
anuxtōe daēnaiiāi	to speak according to the Religion,
anuuarštōe daēnaiiāi	to act according to the Religion,
yaṯ ×ās[1a] *vīspahe aŋhōuš astuuatō*	so that he was among all corporeal life
ašəm ašauuastəmō	the most truthful one in truth,
xšaϑrəm huxšaϑrō.təmō[2]	the best ruling in rule,
raēm raēuuastəmō	the most splendid in splendour,
xᵛarənō[2a] *xᵛarənaŋᵛhastəmō*[3]	the most glorious in glory,
[4] *vərəϑra vərəϑrauuastəmō*[4]	the most victorious in victory.'

80. *vaēnəmnəm ahmaṯ para daēuua pataiiən*	'Before his time the demons used to rush about visibly,
vaēnəmnəm maiiå frāuuōiṯ[1]	their pleasures of lust used to take
vaēnəmnəm ×apa.karšaiiən[1a]	place visibly, visibly they used to drag
jainīš[1b] *haca mašiiākaēibiiō*[1c]	away the women from their men, and

āaṯ tā̊ snaoδəntīš[1d] gərəzānā̊   the demons used to subject to violence
    hazō ×niuuərəziiaiiən[2] daēuua   these crying and lamenting (women).'

81. āaṯ tē aēuuō[1a] ahunō vairiiō   'But a single Ahuna–Vairiia(–Prayer)
    yim ×ašauua ×zaraϑuštrō[1b]   which truthful Zaraϑuštra
        frasrāuuaiiaṯ   recited,
    vī.bərəϑβəṇtəm[1c] āxtūirīm[1d]   divided four times into sections, the
    aparəm[1e] xraoždiiehiia[1] frasrūiti[1f]   last (section) with louder recitation,
    ×zəmarəgūzō[2] auuazaṯ[2a] vīspe[2b]   drove all demons, which are
        daēuua   unworthy of veneration, unworthy
    aiiesniia[2c] auuahmiia[2d]   of praise, under the earth.'

82. yeṅhe[1a] taṯ xᵛarənō isaṯ[1]   'His (= Zaraϑuštras) Glory
    mairiiō tuiriiō[1b] fraŋrase   the Turanian villain Fraŋrasiian desired
    vīspāiš auui[2] karšuuąn[3]yāiš hapta[3]   in all seven climes.
pairi yāiš hapta karšuuąn   Through the seven climes
    mairiiō apataṯ[4] fraŋrase   stormed the villain Fraŋrasiian
    isō xᵛarənō zaraϑuštrāi[4a]   desiring the Glory of Zaraϑuštra.
ā taṯ xᵛarənō frazgaδata[5]   He dashed forward to the Glory,
    auui +viią[6] vītāpəm[7]   chasing after it over the wide waters:
    iṇja mē[7a] uruuisiiatəm[8]   "Iṇja! Turn towards me!" —
aēzō +jasaṯ +təm[9] aēzahe[9a]   "The desire of the one who desired
    yaϑa kaϑaca tē[10] ās zaošō   approached him just as it was the
    mana yaṯ ahurahe mazdā̊   pleasure of me, Ahura Mazdā,
    daēnaiiā̊sca[10a] māzdaiiasnōiš   and of the Mazdayasnian Religion."
ahe raiia ...(= Yt 19.13) ...   On account of his splendour ...
...tā̊scā yazamaide   and these (female Entities) we worship.'

Karde XIII

83. uγrəm kauuaēm [(= Yt 19.9)   'We worship the mighty Glory of the
        xᵛarənō   Kauui–dynasty
    mazdaδātəm yazamaide   created by Mazdā,
    aš.vaṇdrəm[1] uparō.kairīm   the highly praised, supreme worker,

ϑamnaŋ^vhantəm² varəcaŋ^vhantəm³   determined, energetic,
  yaoxštiuuantəm   skilful,
  taraδātəm⁴] aṅiiāiš dāmąn   overcoming the other creatures.'

84. yaṯ upaŋhacaṯ¹ᵃ kauuaēm   'Which accompanied Kauui
   vīštāspəm¹ᵇ   Vīštāspa
  anumatōē daēnaiiāi   to think according to the Religion,
  anuxtōē daēnaiiāi   to speak according to the Religion,
  anuuarštōē daēnaiiāi   to act according to the Religion,
  yaṯ imąm¹ daēnąm¹ᶜ āstaota   so that he confessed to this Religion
  dušmaṅiium² siždiiō³ ˣdaēuuą³ᵃ   chasing away the enemy, driving away
   ˣapaśauuą³ᵇ   the demons.'

85. yō druca¹ ˣpauruuąnaca²   '(He,) who with bow and arrow
   ašāi³ rauuō³ ˣiiaēša⁴   made space for Truth;
  yō druca [(= Yt 13.99) ⁺pauruuąnaca²   (he,) who with bow and arrow
   ašāi rauuō ⁺viuuaēδa²ᵃ   found space for Truth;
  yō bāzušca upastaca   (he,) who served as arm and support
  vīsata aṅhå̊⁵ daēnaiiå̊   of this Religion,
  yaṯ ˣāhurōiš⁵ᵃ zaraϑuštrōiš]   the Ahurian, the Zarathushtrian.'

86. [(= Yt 13.100) yō hīm stātąm¹   '(He,) who led her who was stationary
   hitąm² haitīm³   and fettered
  uzuuažaṯ⁴ haca hinūiβiiō⁵   out of her fetters; he placed her as one
  nī hīm dasta maiδiiōišāδəm⁶   sitting in the middle, giving orders with
  bərəzi.rāzəm ˣafrakauuaitīm⁷   raised voice, being in the first line of
   ašaonīm   battle array, the truthful one,
  ϑrafδąm⁸ gə̄ušca vāstraheca   thriving with cow and pasture,
  friϑąm⁹] gə̄ušca vāstraheca⁶   rejoicing in cow and pasture.'

87. bauuaṯ¹ᵃ aiβi.vaṅiiå̊   'Brave Kauui Vīštāspa
  yasə¹ taxmō kauua¹ᵇ vīštāspō   was victorious over
  tąϑriiāuuantəm² duždaēnəm²ᵃ   evil-minded Tąϑriiāuuant
  pəšanəmca³ daēuuaiiasnəm   and over Pešana, worshipper of demons,
  druuantəmca arəjaṯ.aspəm³ᵃ   and over deceitful Arəjaṯ.aspa,
  uta aṅiiå̊sciṯ³ᵇ aγa   and over the other evil,

dužuuaṇdrauuō x́iiaonā̊ŋhō   malicious X́iiaonas.

ahe raiia ... (= Yt 19.13)   On account of his splendour ...

... tā̊scā yazamaide   and these (female Entities) we worship.'

Karde XIV

88. uγrəm kauuaēm [(= Yt 19.9)   'We worship the mighty Glory of the
        x^varənō   Kauui–dynasty

     mazdaδātəm yazamaide   created by Mazdā,

     aš.vaṇdrəm¹ uparō.kairīm   the highly praised, supreme worker,

     ϑamnaŋ^vhaṇtəm² varəcaŋ^vhaṇtəm³   determined, energetic,
       yaoxštiuuaṇtəm   skilful,

     taraδātəm⁴] aniiāiš dāmąn   overcoming the other creatures.'

89. yaṯ upaŋhacaṯ saošiiaṇtąm¹   'Which will accompany the Victorious
        vərəϑrājanəm   one among the Saviours

     uta aniiā̊sciṯ haxaiiō   and also his other companions,

     ²yaṯ kərənauuāṯ frašəm ahum   so that he will make life excellent,
       +azarəsəntəm³ ×amarəšaṇtəm⁴   ageless, without decay,

     afriϑiiaṇtəm⁵ apuiiaṇtəm   not rotting, not putrefying,

     yauuaējīm⁵ᵃ yauuaēsūm⁵ᵇ   living forever, thriving forever,
       vasō.xšaϑrəm   ruling as it wishes.

     yaṯ irista paiti ×usəhištən⁶   When the dead will rise, (then) will
       jasāṯ juuaiiō⁷ amərəxtiš   come the one without decay reviving
       daϑaite⁸ frašəm vasna⁹ aŋhuš   (the dead) (and) life will create excel-
                                                  lent things according to its own wish.'

90. būn¹ [(= Yt 19.12) gaēϑå̄   'The world of Truth will be
       amaršaṇtīš²   undecaying

     yå̄ ašahe saŋ^vhaitīš   from generation to generation.

     +niš +taṯ³ paiti druxš nāšāite⁴   Falsehood will be returned to the place

     yaδāṯ aiβicit jaγmaṯ   where it had come from

     ašauuanəm mahrkaϑāi   to destroy the truthful one, himself, his

     aom ciϑrəmca⁵ stīmca⁶   family and existence. The (female) vil-

     ā̊vaṯca⁷] ×maire¹ᵃ·² nāšātaēca²   lain will be terrified and the lawless
       mairiiō³ aϑa⁴ ×aratuš⁴ᵃ   (male) villain will disappear.'

ahe raiia ... (= Yt 19.13) ...   On account of his splendour ...
... *tā̊scā yazamaide*   and these (female Entities) we worship.'

Karde XIV

91. *uγrəm kauuaēm* [(= Yt 19.9)   'We worship the mighty Glory
       xᵛarənō   of the Kauui–dynasty
     mazdaδātəm yazamaide   created by Mazdā,
     aš.vandrəm¹ uparō.kairīm   the highly praised, supreme worker,
     ϑamnaηᵛhantəm² varəcaηᵛhantəm³   determined, energetic,
       yaoxštiuuantəm   skilful,
     taraδātəm⁴] *aṇiiāiš dāmąn*   overcoming the other creatures.'

92. *yat astuuat̰.ərətō fraxštāite¹*   'When Astuuat̰.ərəta steps forth
     haca apat̰ kąsaoiiāt̰²   from Lake Kąsaoiia —
     aštō³ mazdā̊ ahurahe   the messenger of Ahura Mazdā,
     ×vīspa.tauruuairiiā̊⁴ puϑrō   the son of Vīspa.tauruuairī,
     vaēδəm⁵ vaējō⁶ yim vārəϑraγnəm⁷   brandishing the victorious missile,
     yim barat̰ taxmō ϑraētaonō   which brave Θraētaona bore
     yat̰ ažiš dahākō jaini⁸   when the Dragon Dahāka was slain,'

93. *yim barat̰ fraηrase turō¹ᵃ*   'which Fraηrasiian the Turanian bore
       yat̰ druuā̊ zainigāuš¹ jaini   when deceitful Zainigau was
       yim barat̰ kauua haosrauua   slain, which Kauui Haosrauuah bore when
       yat̰ turō¹ᵃ jaini fraηrase   Fraηrasiian the Turanian was slain,
     yim barat̰ kauua vīštāspō   which Kauui Vīštāspa bore when he was
       ašahe ×haēnā̊² ⁺jaēšəmnō³   to defeat the armies of the enemies of
     ×tā̊⁴ auuaδa⁵ drujəm nižbarāt̰⁶   Truth; — there, by means of this, he
       ašahe haca gaēϑābiiō   (= Astuuat̰.ərəta) will drive out False-
                                            hood from the world of Truth.'

94. *hō¹ diδāt̰² xratəuš³ ⁺dōiϑrābiia⁴*   'He will gaze with eyes of insight.
     vīspa⁵ dāmąn paiti vaēnāt̰⁶   He will look at all creatures belonging
       ⁺pasca ×išō⁷ ⁺dušciϑraiiā̊⁸   to the one of evil origin, then attack.
     hō vīspəm ahum astuuantəm   At all corporeal life he will
       ižaiiā̊⁹ vaēnāt̰¹⁰ dōiϑrābiia¹¹   gaze with eyes that render strength,

[×]darəšca[12] davǎt̰ [×]amarəxšiiaṇtīm[13]
   vīspąm yąm astuuaitīm gaēϑąm

'and his gaze will render the whole
corporeal world indestructible.'

95. aṅhe[1] haxaiiō[2] [×]frāiieiṇti[3]
   astuuat̰.ərətahe[3a] vərəϑraɣnō
   humanaṇhō[4] huuacaṇhō
   huš́iiaoϑnǎṇhō huδaēna[5]
   naēδa.cit̰[6] [×]miϑō.aojaṇhō[7]
aēšąm x^vaēpaiϑiia[8] hizuuō[9]
   aēšu[10] parō[11] frānāmāite[12]
   aēšmō [×]xruui.druš[13] dušx^varənǎ
vanāt̰[14] aša[15] akąm drujim
   yąm dušciϑrąm təmaṇhaēnīm

'Advancing are the companions
of Victorious Astuuat̰.ərəta,
whose thoughts are good, whose words
are good, whose deeds are good, whose
faith is good; their own tongues,
when they do speak, they utter not
the slightest word of wrong.
And before them will flee
Rage whose attack is cruel, luckless.
He (Astuuat̰.ərəta) will overcome by
Truth the wicked Falsehood of evil
origin, which consists of darkness.'

96. [×]vanaite[1a] akəmcit̰ manō
   vohu manō tat̰ vanaiti[1]
[×]vanaite[1a] miϑaoxtō[2] [×]vāxš[3]
   ərəžuxδō vāxš təm vanaiti
vanāt̰[4] hauruuǎsca[5] amərətǎsca
   uua[6] šuδəmca[7] taršnəmca[8]
vanāt̰ hauruuǎsca amərətǎsca
   aɣəm šuδəmca[9] taršnəmca[10]
[×]frānāmāite[11] dužuuarštāuuarš[12]
   aŋrō mańiiuš [×]axšaiiamnō[13]
ahe raiia . . . (= Yt 19.13) . . .
. . . tǎscā yazamaide

'Evil Thought is overcome,
Good Thought overcomes it.
The falsely spoken Word is overcome
the rightly spoken Word overcomes it.
Wholeness and Immortality will over-
come both Hunger and Thirst.
Wholeness and Immortality will over-
come evil Hunger and Thirst.
The worker of evil deeds,
the Evil Spirit will retreat, powerless.
On account of his splendour . . .
and these (female) Entities we worship.'

Glossary

Alphabetical order:

a ā ā̊ ą ə ə̄ e ē o ō i ī u ū   k x x́ xᵛ g γ c j t ϑ d δ ṱ p f b β
η ή ηᵛ n ń ṇ m   v r š s z š ž ŕ y h.

a- dem.pron. 'this one'

aēuua- numeral 'one'

aēuuaṇdasa- ordinal number, adj.
    'eleventh'

aēta- dem.pron. 'this one'

aēm, aēšąm, aēšu dem.pron. → i-

aēza- adj. 'desiring'

aēzah- ntr. 'desire'

aēšma- m. 'Rage'

aoj 'to speak', pres. aoja-

aojah- ntr. 'strength'

aojišta- superl. 'the mightiest'

aota- ntr. 'cold, frost'

aom acc.sg. → auua-

aiiapta- ntr. 'boon'

aiiah- ntr. 'metal, pot'

aiiesniia- adj. 'unworthy of veneration'

aiϑiiejah- adj. 'free from danger'

aipi prep.+ acc. 'over'

aipi.vohu- personal name of a Kavi

aiβi.gāma- m. 'year'

aiβi.vańiiah- adj. 'overcoming'

aiβiiāxštar- m. 'guardian'

aiβiiāma- 'attacking, aggressive'

aiβitō prep.+ acc. 'around, from
    all sides'

aiβiti- f. 'walking on'

airiia- adj. 'Aryan'

auua- dem.pron. 'that one'

auuaēnaṇt- adj. 'not seeing' (→ vaēn)

auuaϑa adv. 'thus'

auuaδa adv. 'there'

auuaδāṱ adv. 'from there'

auuah- ntr. 'help'

auuahmiia- adj. 'unworthy of praise'

auui prep. 'to, unto'

auruua- adj. 'swift'

auruuaṱ.aspa- adj. 'who has swift
    horses', epithet of Apąm Napāt

aka- adj. 'evil'

axᵛafniia- adj. 'who is without sleep,
    unsleeping'

axᵛarəta- adj. 'shining, gleaming'
    (< *ā-huar-ta-)

axšaiiamna- adj. 'without power,
    powerless'

aγa- adj. 'bad, evil'

aγraēraϑa- m. personal name

ajiiamna- adj. 'undiminishing'

aϑa adv. 'thus'

aϑauruuan- m. 'priest'

aϑra adv. 'there'

aδa adv. 'then, thereupon'

aδāṱ adv. 'then'

aδutauuah- m. name of a mountain

aṱ in Yt 19.46 paiti aṱ < *paiti i̯aṱ

ap- f. 'water'

apa.dis- adj. 'turning away' (?)

apaiia adv. 'thereafter'

apaγžāra- m. 'inlet'

apana- adj. 'distant', ntr. 'final point,
    end'

apara- adj. 'posterior, later'

apastanaηhō Yt 19.42 meaning unclear

apāϑa Yt 19.48 1.sg.subj.aor.act.(?)
    → pad

apərənāiiu- ntr. 'minor age, minority'

apuiiaṇt- adj. 'not putrefying'

afrakauuaṇt- adj. 'being in the first line of battle array'

afrakatac- adj. 'running in the first battle–line'

afrapatāi Yt 19.50 → *pat*

afriϑiiaṇt- adj. 'not rotting'

abda- adj. 'marvellous, wonderful'

aβždānuuan- m. 'water–stream'

aŋra- adj. 'evil'

aŋhaošəmna- adj. 'not drying up'

aŋhaiϑiia- adj. 'untrue'

aŋhuš → *ahu-*

ana instr.sg. → *a-*

anairiia- adj. 'non–Aryan'

anādruxti- f. 'not–lying'

anu prep.+ acc. 'along'

anuuaršti- f. 'acting accordingly'

anuxti- f. 'speaking accordingly'

anumati- f. 'thinking accordingly'

aníia- adj. 'other'

aṇtarə.kaŋha- m. name of a mountain

aṇtarə.daŋhu- m. name of a mountain

ama- m. 'impetuosity'

amaēniɣna- ntr. 'defeat (of enemies) in (their) attack'

×*amarəxšiiaṇt-* adj. 'indestructible'

amarəšáṇt- adj. 'not decaying, without decay' (< *a–mərəč–i̯a–nt-)*

amərəxti- adj. 'who has no decay, undecaying'

amərətatāt- f. 'immortality'

aməša- adj. 'immortal' (< *amə́rta- < *a–mŕ̥–ta-)*

amuiiamna- adj. 'unwavering'

auuanəmna- adj. 'invincible'

aratu- adj. 'who has no rule, lawless' (?)

araska- m. 'envy'

arəjaṯ.aspa- m. personal name

arəδah- ntr. 'side, half'

arəza- m. 'battle' → *gatō.arəza-*

arəzō.šamana- m. personal name

¹*aršan-* m. 'man, hero'

²*aršan-* m. personal name of a Kavi

aša- ntr. 'Truth'

aša.stəmbana- m. name of a mountain

ašauuan- adj. 'truthful'

ašauuastəma- adj.superl. 'most truthful'

aši- f. 'Reward' (< *ár–ti-)*

asaiiā- f. name of a mountain

×*asanuuaṇt-* m. name of a mountain

asəŋgō.gauua- adj. 'whose hands are of stone'

astuuaṯ.ərəta- m. name of a Saošiiaṇt

astuuaṇt- adj. 'corporeal'

aspa- m. 'horse'
  plur. in Yt 19.77 'chariot race' (?)

aspō.gar- 'horse–devouring'

asman- m. 'sky'

az 'to drive', pres. *aza-*
  auua–az 'drive down'

⁺*azarəsaṇt-* adj. 'not ageing, ageless'

azāta- adj. 'unborn'

azinauuaṇt- → *urupi.azinauuaṇt*

aš.pairika- adj. 'accompanied by powerful witches'

aš.vaṇdra- adj. 'highly praised'

aš.varəcah- adj. 'very strong'

ašta- m. 'messenger'

ašta.auruuaṇt- m. name of a mountain

ašta.vašan- m. name of a mountain

aštəma- ordinal number, adj. 'eighth'

aži- m. 'serpent, dragon'

ašáta- 'unhappy' (< *a–či̯ā–ta-)*

¹*ah* 'to be', + gen. 'to belong to', pres. *ah-*

²*ah* 'to throw', pres. *aŋha-* (< *ah–i̯a-)*

para–ah 'to upset, to spill'
ni–ah 'throw down',
    part.med. *niiaṅhəmnō*
ahe, ahmat̰ → *a-*
ahu- m. 'life', nom.sg. *aŋhuš*
ahuna- adj. 'containing the word *ahū*',
    name of the prayer beginning with
    yaϑā ahū vairiiō
ahura- m. 'lord'
ahuraδāta- adj. 'created by the lord'
ahurana- m. name of a mountain

ā postp. and prep.+ acc. 'to, towards'
āat̰ adv. 'then'
āi interjection 'o!'
āuuōiia interjection 'woe!'
āxtūirīm adv. 'four times'
ātar- m. 'fire'
āϑ 'to be terrified',
    aor. (or pres.?) *āϑ-*
āϑβiiāni- adj. 'stemming from Āϑβiia'
āϑritīm adv. 'for the third time'
    → *ϑritiia-*
ādarana- m. name of a mountain
āt̰bitīm adv. 'for the second time'
    → *bitiia-*
āpəm acc.sg. 'water' → *ap-*
ārštiiō.barəz- f. 'height of a spear'
āsitō.gātu- adj. 'lying on the bed'
āsišta- adj.superl. 'swiftest'
āsna- adj. 'noble'
āhuiri- adj. 'Ahurian, lordly'
āhūiriia- adj. 'Ahurian, lordly'

azō.buj- adj. 'rescuing from trouble'
ərəɣaṇt- adj. 'tumultuous'
ərəδβō.zəŋga- adj. 'always on its feet'
ərəzifiia- m. name of a mountain
ərəziša- m. name of a mountain
ərəzī- f. name of a river

ərəzura- m. name of a mountain
ərəžuxδa- adj. 'rightly spoken'

i 'to go', pres. *e-*
    + *frā* 'step forward, advance'
    desid. *iša-* 'attack' in Yt 19.94:
    ×*išō* nom.sg.pres.part.act. (?)
i- dem.pron. 'this'
×*iiaēša* → ¹*iš*
iϑa adv. 'thus, in this way'
iδa adv. 'here'
iṇja adv. interjection
irista- perf.part.pass. → ¹*riϑ*
isaṇt- pres.part.act. → ¹*iš*
iz 'to desire', pres. *iziia-*
¹*iš* 'seek for, wish', pres. *isa-*,
    perf. *iiaēš-*: ×*iiaēša* 3.sg.act.
²*iš* 'set in motion'
    išta- perf.part.pass.
    + *frā* 'send forth, drive off'
išå̄ŋhaēta Yt 19.53 → *han*
×*išō* Yt 19.94 → *i* 'to go'
iškata- m. epithet of mountain
    Upāiri.saēna
išta- f. 'prosperity'
ižā- f. 'strengthening, refreshment'

uiie nom./acc.du.fem. or ntr. → *uua-*
uiti adv. 'thus'
uua- adj. 'both'
uuaiia- adj. 'both'
uɣra- adj. 'powerful, mighty'
uta conj. 'and'
udriia- m. name of a mountain
upa prep. + acc. 'upon'
upaošaŋᵛha- adj. 'eastern'
upairi postpos. and prep.
    + acc. 'upon, on'
uparatāt- f. 'superiority'
uparō.kairiia- adj. 'supreme worker'
upastā- f. 'support'

upāiri.saēna- m. name of a mountain
upāpa- adj. 'living in the waters'
uruuan- m. 'soul'
uruuarā- f. 'plant'
uruuā- f. name of a river, Yt 19.67:
   uruuaδca pleonastic spelling
uruuāxra- ntr. 'heat'
uruuisiiata- adj. 'to be turned towards'
urupi.azinauuaṇt- f. 'bearing the skin
   of a fox', name of a mythical king
uruńiiō.vāiδimiδkā- f. name of

a mountain
[×]*usaoma-* m. name of a mountain
usaδan- m. name of a Kavi
⁺*usaδā-* f. name of a mountain
usca adv. 'away'
uši.darəna- m. name of a mountain
ušta.x^varənah- m. name of a mountain
uštauuaitī- f. name of a river
uštăna- m. (ntr.) 'life, vitality'
uštānō.cinahiia- ntr. 'love of life'
uštra- m. 'camel'

ka- 1. interr.pron. 'who?'; 2. with °*cit̰*:
   indef.pron. 'whoever, everybody'
kaēnan- adj. 'avenging'
kaoirisa- m. name of a mountain
kaofa- m. 'mountain'
kauuai- m. 1. title of pre–Zoroastrian
   priests; 2. title of rulers of a dynasty
   founded by Kauuāta
kauuaiia- adj. 'belonging to the rulers
   of the Kavi–dynasty'
kauuāta- m. name of a Kavi
kakahiiu- m. name of a mountain
katāra- 1. interrog.adj. 'who or which
   of two?'; 2. with °*cit̰*: indef. adj.
   'each one out of two'
kaϑa adv. 'how?'
kadruua.aspa- m. name of a mountain
kar 'to make', pres. *kərənao-*
karapan- m. title of an anti–Zoroastrian
   priest
karan- m. 'edge'
karš 'to drag', pres. *karša-*
   + *apa* 'drag away'
karšuuar-/karšuuan- ntr. 'clime'
kāuuaiia- adj. 'belonging to the rulers
   of the Kavi–dynasty'
kasaoiia- name of Lake Hāmūn in

Sīstān
kasō.tafəδrā- f. name of a mountain
kərəsa- m. 'robber'
kərəsauuazdah- m. name of
   Fraŋrasiian's brother
kərəsāspa- m. name of a mythical hero
kəhrp- f. 'form, shape, body'
x́iiaona- adj. name of enemies
   of the Avesta–people

xraoždiiah- adj.comp. 'louder'
xratu- m. 'mental power, insight'
xruui.dru- adj. 'attacking cruelly',
   epithet of Rage (*aēšma-*)
xruuišiiaṇt- adj. 'blood–thirsty'
xšaēta- adj. 'shining'
xšaϑra- ntr. 'rule, reign'
xšaϑriia- adj. 'ruling'
xšā 'to rule', pres. *xšaiia-*
xšōiϑnī- fem. → *xšaēta-*
xšuuaēpā- f. 'tail'
xšuδra- adj. 'liquid'
xštuua- ordinal number, adj. 'sixth'
x^vaēpaiϑiia- adj. 'own'
x^vairiia- adj. 'to be eaten, edible'
x^varəϑa- ntr. 'food'
x^varənaŋ^vhaitī- f. name of a river

x^varənaŋʷhaṇt- adj. 'splendid'

x^varənaŋʷhastəma- adj.superl. 'most splendid'

x^varənah- ntr. 'glory'

x^vāstrā- f. name of a river

x^vid 'to sweat', pres. x^vīsa-

gaēiϑiia- adj. 'corporeal'

gaēϑā- f. 'living being', 'world' (sg. and plur.)

gaiia- m. 'life'

gairi- m. 'mountain'

gairišac- adj. 'following the slope'

gau- m./f. 1. 'ox, cow'; 2. 'milk'

gauua- m. 'hand' (of daēvic creatures)

gatō.arəza- adj. 'whose battle has come, has been joined' (?)

gaṇdarəβa- m. name of a mythical monster

gam 'to go, to come', pres. jasa-, perf. jaγm-
+ həm 'come together'
+ aiβi-cit̰ 'come to'

gar- f. 'welcome'
garō nmāna- 'House of Welcome'

garəma- ntr. 'heat'

gərəz 'to lament', pres. gərəz-

gufra- adj. 'deep, unfathomable'

grab 'to grab, grasp, seize', pres. gəuruuaiia-, aor. gərəfš-
+ paiti apa 'to withdraw'
+ ham 'to grap, grasp, seize'

-ca enclitic particle 'and'

caxra- m. 'wheel'

cavϑβar- cardinal number, adj. 'four'

cavϑβarəsaṇt- cardinal number, adj. 'forty'

carətā- f. 'racecourse'

ciϑra- ntr. 'offspring'

-cit̰ enclitic particle

cinman- ntr. 'desire, endeavour'; cinmāne them.loc.sg.

jaini 3.sg.pass. → jan

jaini- f. 'woman'

jaγāuru- adj. 'awake'

+jaēšəmnō Yt 19.93 → ji

jafra- adj. 'deep'

jan 'to slay, kill', pres. jana-
+ auua 'strike down'

ji 'to defeat', fut. jaēšiia-:
+jaēšəmnō nom.sg.m.part.med.

jiγāuru- adj. 'awake'

jira- adj. 'lively'

jīv 'to live', pres.caus. juuaiia- 'make alive, revive'

juuaiiō nom.sg.m.pres.part.act. → jīv

ta- dem.pron. 'this'

taēra- m. 'peak'

taxma- adj. 'brave, heroic, strong'

tac 'rush along', pres. taca-
+ auui ham 'come together into'
+ apa 'rush away'

tataša Yt 19.52 → taš

tap 'be hot', pres.inchoat. tafsa- 'become hot'

tanū- f. 'body'

taraδāt- adj. 'overcoming'

tarō.yāra- adj. 'lasting over the years'

taršu- adj. 'dry, solid'

taršta- perf.part.pass. of ϑrah 'to be afraid'

taršna- m. 'thirst'

taš 'to fashion', perf. tataš-

tq̇ϑriiāuuaṇt- m. name of an enemy of Vīštāspa

təmaŋhaēna- adj. 'consisting of darkness'

te pers.pron. → tŭm

tiṇja adv. interjection

tŭiriia- adj. 'Turanian'

tuδaskā- f. name of a mountain

tŭra- adj. 'Turanian'

tū enclitic particle

tŭm pers.pron.2.sg. 'you'
 ϑβąm acc.sg.
 te (enclit.) dat.sg.

ϑanj 'to drag, pull', pres. *ϑanjaiia*-

ϑamnaŋᵛhant- adj. 'determined'

ϑβarəxštar- m. 'fashioner'

ϑβaj 'to become oppressed',
 pres. *ϑβązja*-

ϑβąm → *tŭm*

ϑrāϑra- ntr. 'protection'

ϑrąp- f. 'contentment'

ϑrafδa- adj. 'thriving'

ϑritiia- ordinal number, adj. 'third'

ϑrisant- cardinal number, adj. 'thirty'

ϑrizafan- adj. 'three-mouthed'

ϑrizafah- adj. 'three-mouthed'

ϑrišuua- ntr. 'third'

daēuua- m. 'demon'

daēuuaiiasna- adj. 'worshipping
 demons'

daēuuō.dāta- adj. 'created by demons'

daēnā- f. 'view, attitude, religion'

daoiϑrī- f. 'speech' (of daevic
 creatures), 'rant'

daožaŋᵛha- ntr. 'hell'

dauu 'to speak' (of daevic creatures),
 'to gabble', pres. *dauua*-

daŋra- adj. 'knowledgeable'

daŋhu- f. 'land; inhabitant'

daŋhupaiti- m. 'lord of lands'

dar 'to hold', pres. *dāra*-
 + *ni* 'to keep oneself hidden'

darəγa- adj. 'long'

darəγō.jīti- f. 'long life'

darši.kairiia- adj. 'acting audaciously'

dasəma- ordinal number, adj. 'tenth'

dasta → *dā*

dahāka- m. name of a mythical
 dragon (*aži*-)

dā 'to give'; 'to place, create'
 pres. *daϑā-/daϑ*-, *daϑa*- (them.),
 perf. *daδā-/daδ*-
 dasta 3.sg.inj.pres.med.

dātar- m. 'creator'

dānaiiana- adj. 'descending from Dāna'

dāman- ntr. 'creature'

dāru- ntr. 'wood', also:
 'spear' in Yt 19.42 (?),
 'bow' in Yt 19.85 (?)

dāštaiiāni- m. personal name

dərəs- f. 'gaze'

dōuš.manahiia- ntr. 'evil-mindedness'

dōiϑra- ntr. 'eye'

di- dem.pron., only enclit. acc.

dis 'to show', pres. *daēsaiia*-
 + *ham* 'show to oneself, bear
 in mind'

dī 'to see, behold', pres. *diδā*-

duua- cardinal number, adj. 'two'

duuadasa- ordinal number,
 adj. 'twelfth'

duuar 'go, run, rush' (of daevic creatures), pres. *duuara*-
 + *frā̆* 'run forward'
 + *hąm* 'run (to the contest)'

dušxᵛarənah- adj. 'whose *xᵛarənah*-
 is evil, luckless'

dušciϑra- adj. 'of evil origin'

dušmańiiu- adj. 'evil-minded, enemy'

dužuuaṇdru- adj. 'malicious'

dužuuarštāuuarəz- adj. 'doing bad
 work'

duždaēna- adj. 'of evil faith, evil-
 minded'

draoγa- adj. 'false'

draonah- ntr. 'portion, share'

draošišuuaṇt- m. name of a mountain

druua- adj. 'robust, healthy'

druuatāt- f. 'health'

druuaṇt- adj. 'deceitful'

dru–ca Yt 19.85 instr.sg. of
→ *dāru-* (?)

druj- f. 'falsehood'

⁺*t̰biṣaiiaṇt-* adj. 'inimical, foe'

paoiriia- adj. 'first'

paoirī- fem. → *pauru-*

paoirīm adv. 'for the first time'

paiti prep. and postp.
+ acc. 'to, towards, against'
+ instr. 'on, upon'
+ gen. 'for'
+ loc. 'for, in, at'

paitiša- adj. 'hostile'

pairi prep. + acc. 'around'

pairikā- f. 'witch'

pauru- adj. 'many, numerous'

pauruuata- m. 'mountain, rock'

pauruuan- ntr. 'knot, joint (of reed)',
also: 'arrow' (?) in Yt 19.85

pauruuaṇa-ca Yt 19.85 instr.sg.
→ *pauruuan-*

pac 'to cook', pres. *paca*

pat 'fly, rush; fall; go' (of daevic
creatures), pres. *pata-*,
pres.caus. *pataiia-*
+ ă 'rush about'
+ *auua* 'go down'
+ *us* 'go up', caus.: 'raise up'
+ ă *frā* 'walk about'

pavॢana- m. personal name.

pad 'to fall', root-aor. *pav̰-* (?)
+ *frā* ă 'fall upon' → *apāv̰a*

paṇcō.hiia- adj. 'of five species'

paṇtān- m. 'path'

para prep. + abl. 'before'

paraδāta- adj. 'created before',
epithet of Haošiiaŋha

⁺*parā̊ṅhāt̰* 3.sg.subj.pres.act. → ²*ah*

parā̊nc- Adj. 'away, aside'

parā̊š Nom.sg.m. → *parā̊nc-*

parō adv. 'formerly'
prep. + abl. 'on account of
postp. + loc. 'before'

part 'to fight, struggle', pres. *parəta-*
+ *paiti* 'fight against'

pasu- m. 'cattle'

paskāt̰ adv. 'from behind'

pasca adv. temporal 'then'

pascaēta adv. temporal 'then'

pārəntara- adj. 'opposite, other'

pərənāiiu- adj. 'of full age, majority'

pəšana- m. personal name

pouru.xšnut- f. 'much strengthening'

pouru–ca acc.pl.ntr. → *pauru-*

pouru.vāstra- adj. 'rich in pastures'

pouruš.xᵛāstra- adj. 'granting much
well-being'

pi 'to swell, surge', pres. *pinuua-*
+ *frā̆* 'to swell, surge forward'

pitaona- m. personal name

pitar- m. 'father', nom.sg. *ptā-ca*

pitu- m. 'meal'

pisina- m. name of a Kavi

puθra- m. 'son'

fraēštō Yt 19.34 → ²*iš*

fraorəpa- m. 'mountain' (?)

fraxšni- adj. 'prudent'

fradaθā- f. name of a river

fraŋrasiian- m. personal name

framitəm Yt 19.29 → *mī*

frasasti- f. 'honour'

⟨*fra*⟩*sāna-* ntr. 'destruction'

frasāstar- m. 'master'

frasparat̰ → *spar*
frasrūiti- f. 'recitation'
frazaṇti- f. 'offspring'
fraša- adj. 'excellent'
frašō.carǝtar- m. 'renovator'
frāuuōit̰ 3.sg.opt.pres.act. (by haplo-
    logy < **frā–uuauuōit̰*), → *bū*
frāϑβǝrǝsā̊m gen.pl.
    → *nauua.frāϑβǝrǝsa-*
frāpaiia- adj. 'western'
frāpaiiah- m. name of a mountain
×*frā̊ṇku-* m. 'peak' (< **fra–aṇku-*)
frā̊ṇc- adj. 'turned forward'
frą̄š nom.sg.m. → *frā̊ṇc-*
friϑa- adj. 'rejoicing'
fru 'float, swim', pres.caus. *frāuuaiia-*
    + *us* 'wash away, sweep aside'
fšaoni- f. 'herd'
fšuiiaṇt- adj. 'breeding cattle'

baēšaza- ntr. 'cure'
baiiana- m. name of a mountain
baj 'to distribute, apportion', pres.
    baža-, Yt 19.8 *bažat̰* act. in an im-
    personal sense, lit.: 'one appor-
    tioned (the share to . . .)'
baṇd 'to bind', pres. *baṇdaiia-*
bar 'to bear', med. also: 'to ride',
    pres. *bara-*

    + *us* 'to bring up'
    + *niš* 'to bring away, drive out'
    + *paiti* 'to take up'
barana- m. name of a mountain
barō.sraiian- m. name of a mountain
barō.zuš- adj. 'rejoicing in booty'
bānumaṇt- adj. 'splendid'
bāmiia- adj. 'radiant'
bāzu- m. 'arm'
bǝrǝz- adj. 'lofty'
bǝrǝzaṇt- adj. 'lofty, high'
bǝrǝzi.rāz- adj. 'giving orders with
    raised voice'
biiaršan- m. name of a Kavi
bitiia- ordinal number, adj. 'second'
bitīm adv. 'for the second time'
    → *bitiia-*
bī 'to fear', also: 'to terrify' (?)
    +*biβiuuā̊* nom.sg.m.perf.part.act.
bud 'to perceive', pres. *baoδa-*
buna- m. 'bottom'
bū 'to become', pres. *bauua-*,
    root–aor. *bū-*
    + *pairi* 'to get hold of'
    + *frā̆* 'to take place, happen'
būmiia- m. name of a mountain
būmī- f. 'earth'
bram 'to wander about',
    pres.inchoat. *brāsa-*

naēδa negation 'neither'
naoma- ordinal number, adj. 'ninth'
naire.manah- adj. 'manly–minded'
nairiia- adj. 'manly'
nairiiąm.hąm.varǝitiuuaṇt- adj.
    'skilled in manly defence'
nauua cardinal number, indecl. 'nine'
nauua.frāϑβǝrǝsa- m. 'nine glades'
    Yt 19.77

napāt- m. 'grandson',
    with *apąm* name of a god
naṇhušmaṇt- m. name of a mountain
nam 'to bow', pres. *nǝma-*, *nāma-*
    + *apa* 'to go away'
    + *frā̆* 'to flee, retreat'
nar- m. 'man'
nara- m. 'man'
narauua- adj. 'descending from Naru'

¹*nas* 'to reach', *s*–aor. *nāš-*
  + *niš* 'to take away, return' Yt 19.12
²*nas* 'to be lost, disappear, perish',
  s–aor. *nāš-*
nāman- ntr. 'name'
nərə.gar- adj. 'man–devouring'
nōit̰ negation 'not'
niiaṅhəmnō Yt 19.67 → ²*ah*
niuuika- m. personal name
nipātar- m. 'protector'
nišharətar- m. 'watcher'
nī 'to lead', pres. *naiia-*
  + *auua* 'to fetch down'
nura- adj. 'agile, alert' (?)
nmāna- ntr. 'house'

ma- pers.pron.1.sg. 'I'
  mąm acc.sg.
  mē dat.sg. (enclit.)
  mana gen.sg.
maēnaxa- m. name of a mountain
maiiah- ntr. 'pleasure of lust'
maiδiiōišād- adj. 'sitting in the
  middle'
mairiia- adj. 'wicked, villainous',
  m. 'villain'
maγna- adj. 'naked'
man 'to think', *s*–aor. *maṇh-*
manah- ntr. 'thought'
mańiiauua- adj. 'spiritual'
mańiiu- m. 'spirit'
marəxštar- m. 'former'
marc 'to destroy', *s*–aor. *marəxš-*
mašiia- m. 'mortal, man' (< *mártia-)
mašiiāka- m. 'mortal, man'
masan- ntr. 'greatness'
mazišuuaṇt- m. name of a mountain
mazdaδāta- adj. 'created by Mazdā'
mazdā- m. 'wisdom', with *ahura-*
  name of the highest god of the

Mazdayasnian religion
mahrka- m. 'destruction'
mahrkaϑa- m. 'destruction'
māzaṅiia- adj. 'gigantic'
māzdaiiasni- adj. 'belonging to the
  worshippers of Mazdā,
  Mazdayasnian'
marəiϑiiu- m. 'death'
marəγa- m. 'bird'
marəϑβaṇt- adj. 'thinking of'
miϑaoxta- adj. 'falsely spoken'
miϑō.aojah- adj. 'whose speech
  is false'
miϑra- m. name of a god
mī 'to exchange', perf.part.pass. *mita-*
  + *frǎ* 'to transform'
mrū 'to speak', pres. *mrao-*

va- pers.pron.2.pers. enclitic 'you'
  vō gen. 'of you'
vaēδa- m. 'missile'
vaēn 'to see', pres. *vaēna-*
  + *aiβi* 'to look upon, gaze at'
  + *paiti* 'to look at'
vairi- m. 'bay'
vairiia- adj. 'to be chosen, best'
vaxš 'to grow', pres. *uxša-, uxšiia-*
  + *frǎ* 'to grow forth'
  + *frǎ us* 'to climb up, flare up'
vac- m. 'word, speech'
vacah- ntr. 'word, speech'
ˣ*vafrauuaṇt-* m. name of a mountain
⁺*vafrā-* f. name of a mountain
vaṇhan- ntr. 'goodness'
vaṅhazdā- m. 'giver of the very good'
vaṇhuiiā̊ gen.sg.f. → *vohu-*
van 'to overcome, defeat', pres. *vana-*
  vanaiṇtī- pres.part.act.fem.
vanaiia.barəzan- m. 'height of a tree'
varəcaŋᵛhaṇt- adj. 'energetic'

varəńiia- adj. 'having made his
   (bad) choice'

varəmi- f. 'wave'

⁺*varəzi.dōiϑra-* adj. 'having powerful,
   sharp eyes'

varəšauua- m. personal name

varəz 'to work', pres. *vərəziia-*
   + *ni* 'to subject'

vas 'to wish', perf.part.pass. *ušta-*

vasō.xšaϑra- adj. 'ruling according to
   its own will, as it wishes'

vastra- ntr. 'garment'

vasna- m. 'wish'

vaz 'drive, carry', pres. *vaza-*,
   perf. *vaoz-*
   + *auui hąm* 'to flow into'
   + *uz* 'to lead out'

vahišta- adj. superl. 'best'

vāiti.gaēsa- m. name of a mountain

vāxəδrikā- f. name of a mountain

vārəγna- lit.: 'slaying lambs' (?), only
   with *mərəγā-* 'bird of pray')

vārəϑraγna- adj. 'victorious'

vāša- m. 'chariot' (< **u̯árta-*)

vāstra- ntr. 'pasture'

vāstriia- adj. 'belonging to pasture,
   farming, breeding'; m. 'farmer'

vąϑβā- f. 'cattle'

vərəϑra- ntr. 'victory'

vərəϑrauuan- adj. 'victorious'

vərəϑrauuastəma- adj.superl. 'most
   victorious'

vərəϑraγna- ntr. 'victoriousness'

vərəϑrajan- adj. 'victorious'

vouru.kaša- adj. 'having wide bays',
   name of a mythical lake

vouru.gaoiiaoiti- adj. 'having wide
   cattle–pastures'

vouruša- m. name of a mountain

vohu- adj. 'good'

vō → *va-*

vōiγnā- f. 'flood'

viiarəϑiia- adj. 'undisputed'

viiāxana- adj. 'eloquent'

viiāxman- ntr. 'assembly',
   pres.denom. *viiāxmaniia-*
   'to speak in the assembly

⁺*viią* nom.sg.m.pres.part.act. → *vī*

⁺*viuuaēδa* → *vid*

vij 'to brandish', pres. *vaēja-*

vid 'to find', perf. *viuuaēd-*
   ⁺*viuuaēδa* 3.sg.ind.perf.act.

viδβana- m. name of a mountain

vis 'to be available, serve as', pres. *visa-*

viš- m. 'poisonous plant' (?)

višauuā- f. name of a mountain

vī 'to pursue, chase after'
   + *ā̆* 'to draw near'

vī.bərəϑβənt- adj. 'divided into
   sections'

vīuuaŋhuša- adj. 'son of Vivasvant'

vītāp- f. 'wide water' (?)

vīra- m. 'man'

vīs- f. 'family, clan'

vīspa- adj. 'all, every'

vīspa.tauruuairī- f. name of the mother
   of Astuuaṱ.ərəta

vīspō.aiiāra- adj. 'lasting for all the
   days'

vīzafāra- adj. 'with wide–open mouth'

vīšauuant- adj. 'poisonous'

vīštāspa- m. name of a Kavi

raēuuant- adj. 'opulent, splendid',
   m. name of a mountain

raēuuastəma- adj.superl. 'most
   splendid'

raēmana- m. name of a mountain

raoxšna- adj. 'light, radiant'

raoxšni.xšnut- f. 'radiant strengthen-

ing'
raoδita- m. name of a mountain
raiii- m. 'splendour'
rauuah- ntr. 'space'
ravθa- m. 'chariot'
ravaēštā- m. 'warrior'
rapiϑβina- adj. 'of midday'
raz 'to stretch', pres. *rāzaiia*-
 + *ham* 'to rise up, step (to the

saokā- f. 'glory, standing, reputation'
saošiiaṇt- m. 'saviour'
sata- ntr. 'hundred'
saŋhu- f. 'order, command'
saŋᵛhaṇt- adj. 'from generation
 to generation, continuously'
sāiriuuaṇt- m. name of a mountain
sāstar- m. 'commander'
siiāuuaršan- m. name of a Kavi
siiāmaka- m. name of a mountain
sicidāuua- m. name of a mountain
sižd 'to chase away', pres. *šiždiia*-
sī 'to lie', pres. *saē*-
 + *pairi* 'to extend around'
surunuuata- adj. 'audible'
sūra- adj. 'strong',
 with gen. 'ruling over'
star 'to strike down, lay low',
 perf.part.pass. *stərəta*-
stā 'to stand', pres. *hišta*-, *xšta*-;
 perf. °*šast*-, perf.part.pass. *stāta*-
 + *us paiti* 'to rise up again'
 + *frə̄* 'to step forth'
 + *vī* 'to extend'
 + *ham* 'to rise'
stāta- perf.part.pass. 'standing' → *stā*
stərəta- perf.part.pass. → *star*
sti- f. 'existence'
stu 'to praise', pres. *stao*-

contest)'
razura- ntr. 'forest'
rātā- f. 'gift'
[1]*riϑ* 'to die', perf.part.pass. *irista*-
[2]*riϑ* 'to mix', pres. *raēϑβa*-
ruc 'to shine', pres. *raocaiia*-
 + *us* 'to blaze up'
rud 'to grow', pres. *raoδa*-
 + *ə̆* 'to grow up'

 + *ə̆* 'to confess'
spaētinī- adj. fem. of *spaētita*- 'white'
spar 'to jerk, push, kick', pres. *spara*-
 + *frə̄* 'to kick against' (+ Gen.)
spašiti- f. 'observation'
spā 'to throw', pres. *spaiia*-, *spispa*-
 + *apa* 'to throw away, aside'
spāra.dāšta- adj. 'granting prosperity'
spəṇta- adj. 'bounteous'
spəṇtō.dāta- m. name of a mountain
spitauuarənah- m. name of a mountain
spitāma- adj. name of Zarathushtra's
 family
spitiiura- m. personal name
spiti.dōiϑra- adj. 'having bright eyes'
snāuuiδka- m. personal name
snud 'to cry', pres. *snaoδa*-
sraiian- ntr. 'beauty'
srīra- adj. 'beautiful'
sru 'to hear', pres.caus. *srāuuaiia*-
 + *frə̄* 'to recite'
sruuara- adj. 'bearing (an armour of)
 horn(y scales), horned'
sruuō.zana- adj. 'having leaden jaws'
srut.gaoša- adj. 'having ears which
 hearken'
srut.gaošōtəma- adj.superl. 'having
 ears which hearken best'

zaoϑrā- f. 'libation'

zaoša- m. 'pleasure, liking'

zainigau- m. personal name

zairi.pāšna- adj. 'having a yellow heel'

zairita- adj. 'yellow'

zauuanō.sū- adj. 'who prospers through libations'

zauruuan- m. 'old age'

zaxšaϑra- ntr. 'words of abuse'

zadah- ntr. 'fundament, buttock'

zafar- ntr. 'mouth'

zam- f. 'earth'

zaraϑuštra- m. name of the founder of the Mazdayasnian Religion

zaraϑuštri- adj. 'Zarathushtrian'

zarańiiō.pusa- adj. 'having a golden diadem'

zarənumaitī- f. name of a river

zasta- m. 'hand' (of ahuric beings)

zāta- adj. 'born'

zəmarəguz- adj. 'hiding in the earth'

zərəδaza- m. name of a mountain

zurō.jata- adj. 'treacherously killed'

zuš 'to enjoy', perf.part.pass. *zušta-*
  + *frǎ* 'to like, love'

zgad 'to dash', pres. *zgaδa-*
  + *ǎ frǎ* 'to dash forward to'

zbar 'to go astray, deviate, move around', pres. *zbara-*

zraiiah- ntr. 'lake, sea'

zruuan- m. 'time'

šud- m. 'thirst'

ś(ii)u 'to move, go away', pres.inchoat. *śusa-*
  + *frǎ* 'to fly away'
  pres. *śauua-^{ti}* 'to drive'
  + *apa* 'to drive away'

śiiaoϑna- ntr. 'deed' (< *čiautna-)

ya- rel.pron. 'who'

yaēšiiant- → *yah*

yaoxštiuuant- adj. 'skilful'

yauuaējī- adj. 'living forever'

yauuaēsū- adj. 'thriving forever'

yauuat adv. 'as far as'

yaϑa 1. adv. 'how'; 2. subord.conj.: causal 'because, as'; final 'so that'

yaϑa yat subord.conj. consec. 'so that'

yaϑna adj. 'how'

yaδāt adv. 'where from'

yat 1. adv.; 2. subord.conj.: temp. 'when'; causal 'since'; final, consec. 'so that'

yam 'to hold', pres. *yāsa-* + *ni* 'seize'

yasna- m. 'veneration'

yaz 'to venerate', pres. *yaza-*

yazata- adj. 'adorable'

yah 'to boil', pres. *yaēšiia-*

yahmiia.jatara- m. name of a mountain

yātu- m. 'sorcerer, wizard'

yezi subord.conj. conditional 'if', temp. 'when'

yima- m. name of a mythical king

yimō.kərənta- adj. 'cutting Yima to pieces'

¹*ha-* dem.pron. 'this'

²*ha-* pers.pron.3.pers., enclitic *hē* dat.sg.

haētumata- adj. 'belonging to Haētumaṇt'

haētumaṇt- m. name of a river

haēnā- f. 'enemy army, hostile army'

haoma- m. name of an intoxicating plant

¹*haosrauuah-* m. name of a Kavi

²*haosrauuah-* m. 'Well-famed', name of a bay of Lake Vourukaša

haošiiaŋha- m. name of a mythical king

haitī- pres.part.act.fem. 'being' → ¹*ah*

hauruuatāt- f. 'wholeness'

hakat̲ adv. 'at once'

haxai- m. 'companion'

hac 'to follow, accompany', pres. *haca-* + *upa* 'accompany'

haca prep. + instr. and abl. 'from'

haυϑra adv. 'at once'

haυϑrauuata- ntr. 'immediate victory'

hapta cardinal number, indecl. 'seven'

haptaiϑiia- adj. 'of seven parts'

haptaϑa- ordinal number, adj. 'seventh'

han 'to win', pres.desid. *išā̊ŋha-*

[1]*hama-* adj. 'same'

[2]*hama-* adj. 'all, whole'

hamaṇkuna- adj. 'hooked together'

hamərəϑa- m. 'enemy'

hamō.manah- adj. 'having the same thought, of the same thought'

hamō.vacah- adj. 'having the same speech, of the same speech'

hamō.šiiaoϑnah- adj. 'having the same action, of the same action'

haraitī- f. name of the primordial mountain

harc 'to emit, discharge', pres. *harəcaiia-* + *frā̆* 'to send forth'

hazaŋra- cardinal number, adj. 'thousand'

hazaŋra.yaoxšti- adj. 'having a thousand skills'

hazah- ntr. 'violence'

hāu nom.sg. → *auua-*

hāma- adj. 'all, whole'

hạm.varəiti- f. 'defence'

hạm.varəitiuuaṇt- → *nairiiạm.hạm.varəitiuuaṇt-*

hē → [2]*ha-*

hi 'to bind, fetter', perf.part.pass. *hita-*

hi- pers.pron.3.pers., only enclitic acc.

hita- perf.part.pass. 'fettered' → *hi*

hitāspa- m. personal name

hid 'to drive', pres. *hiδa-* + *apa* 'escape' (fientive sense) in Yt 19.56

hinu- m. 'bond, fetter'

hizū- m. 'tongue'

huuacah- adj. 'whose words are good'

huuaršta- adj. 'well–done'

huuaspā- f. name of a river

huuạ̊ϑβa- adj. 'having good herds'

huuīra- adj. 'manly'

huxšaϑrō.təma- adj. 'whose rule is best'

hutāšta- adj. 'well–created'

huδaēna- adj. 'whose faith is good'

hunu- m. 'son' (of daevic creatures), 'spawn'

humata- adj. 'well–thought'

humanah- adj. 'whose thoughts are good'

husasta- adj. 'well ordered'

huzaṇtu- f. 'good recognition'

hušiiaoϑna- adj. 'whose deeds are good'

hūxta- adj. 'well–spoken'

Select Bibliography

1. Avestan Texts

DARMESTETER, J.: *Le Zend–Avesta*. 3 vols., Paris 1892–93, repr. 1960.

DEHGHAN, K.: *Der Awesta–Text Srōš Yašt (Yasna 57) mit Pahlavi- und Sanskritübersetzung*. München 1982 (*MSS*–Beihefte 11, Neue Folge).

GELDNER, K. F.: *Avesta*. The sacred books of the Parsis, 3 vols., Stuttgart 1896. 1889. 1896.

GELDNER, K. F.: *Drei Yasht aus dem Zendavesta*. Stuttgart 1884.

GERSHEVITCH, I.: *The Avestan Hymn to Mithra*. With an Introduction, Translation and Commentary. Cambridge 1959, repr. 1967.

GERSHEVITCH, I.: "Old Iranian Literature". *Handbuch der Orientalistik* I 4,2, Leiden/Köln 1968, 1–30.

HINTZE, A.: *Der Zamyād–Yašt*. Edition, Übersetzung, Kommentar. Wiesbaden 1994 (Beiträge zur Iranistik 15).

HUMBACH, H.: *The Gāthās of Zarathushtra* and the Other Old Avestan Texts. In collaboration with J. ELFENBEIN and P.O. SKJÆRVØ. Part I: Introduction — Text and Translation. Part II: Commentary. Heidelberg 1991 (Indogermanische Bibliothek: Reihe 1, Lehr- und Handbücher).

HUMBACH, H. and ELFENBEIN, E.: *Ērbedestān*. An Avesta–Pahlavi Text. München 1990 (*MSS*–Beihefte 15, Neue Folge).

INSLER, S.: *The Gāthās of Zarathustra*. Teheran–Liège 1975 (Acta Iranica 8).

JAMASPASA, K. M.: *Aoɡ∂madaēcā*. A Zoroastrian Liturgy. Wien 1982.

JAMASPASA, K. M. and HUMBACH, H.: *Pursišnīhā*. A Zoroastrian Catechism. I. II. Wiesbaden 1971.

KELLENS, J.: *Fravardīn Yašt*. (Yt 13,1–70): Introduction, édition et glossaire. Wiesbaden 1975 (Iranische Texte 6).

KELLENS, J. and PIRART, E.: *Les textes vieil-avestiques*. Wiesbaden. Vol. I: Introduction, texte et traduction. 1988. Vol. II: Répertoires grammaticaux et lexique. 1990. Vol. III: Commentaire. 1991.

LOMMEL, H.: *Die Yäšt's des Awesta*. Göttingen/Leipzig 1927 (Quellen der Religionsgeschichte, Gruppe 6).

MALANDRA, W. W.: *The Fravaši Yašt*. Introduction, Text, Translation and Commentary. Phil.Diss. University of Pennsylvania 1971 (microfilm–xerography).

MONNA, M.C.: *The Gathas of Zarathustra*. A Reconstruction of the text. Amsterdam 1978.

NARTEN, J.: *Der Yasna Haptaŋhāiti*. Wiesbaden 1986.

OETTINGER, N.: *Untersuchungen zur avestischen Sprache am Beispiel des Ardvīsūr–Yašt*. Unpubl. typescript, München 1983.

PANAINO, A.: *Tištrya*. Part I: The Avestan Hymn to Sirius. Roma 1990 (= Serie Orientale Roma LXVIII,1).

PIRART, E.V.: *Kayân Yasn* (Yasht 19.9–96). L'origine avestique des dynasties mythiques d'Iran. Barcelona 1992.

REICHELT, H.: *Avesta Reader*. Texts, notes, glossary and index. Strassburg 1911.

SETHNA, T.R.: *Yashts*. In Roman Script with Translation. Karachi 1976.

TARAF, Z.: *Der Awesta–Text Niyāyiš mit Pahlavi und Sanskritübersetzung*. München 1981 (*MSS*-Beihefte 10, Neue Folge).

WOLFF, F.: *Avesta. Die heiligen Bücher der Parsen*. Übersetzt auf der Grundlage von Chr. Bartholomaes Altiranischem Wörterbuch. Straßburg 1910, repr. Berlin 1960.

2. Avestan Language

BARTHOLOMAE, Chr.: "Vorgeschichte der iranischen Sprachen. Awestasprache und Altpersisch". *Grundriß der Iranischen Philologie*, edited by W. GEIGER and E. KUHN, vol. I, part 1, Straßburg 1895–1901, 1–248.

BARTHOLOMAE, Chr.: *Altiranisches Wörterbuch*. Straßburg 1904.

BEEKES, R.S.P.: *A Grammar of Gatha–Avestan*. Leiden/New York/København/Köln 1988.

DUCHESNE-GUILLEMIN, J.: *Les composés de l'Avesta*. Liège–Paris 1936.

HOFFMANN, K.: "Altiranisch". *Handbuch der Orientalistik* I, IV Iranistik, 1 Linguistik. Leiden/Köln 1958, repr. 1967, 1–19 (= *Aufsätze zur Indoiranistik* vol. I, edited by J. NARTEN, Wiesbaden 1975, 58–76).

HOFFMANN, K.: "Avestan Language". *Encyclopaedia Iranica* III, edited by E. YARSHATER, London/New York 1990, 47–62.

HOFFMANN, K. and NARTEN, J.: *Der Sasanidische Archetypus*. Untersuchungen zu Schreibung und Lautgestalt des Avestischen. Wiesbaden 1989.

JACKSON, A. V. W.: *An Avesta Grammar in Comparison with Sanskrit*. Part I, Stuttgart 1892, repr. New York 1975.

KELLENS, J.: *Les noms–racines de l'Avesta*. Wiesbaden 1974.

KELLENS, J.: *Le verbe avestique*. Wiesbaden 1984.

KELLENS, J.: "Avestique". *Compendium Linguarum Iranicarum*, edited by R. SCHMITT, Wiesbaden 1989, 32–55.

REICHELT, H.: *Awestisches Elementarbuch*. Heidelberg 1909, repr. 1967.

3. Zoroastrianism

BOYCE, M.: *A History of Zoroastrianism*. Leiden/Köln. (*HdO* I 8, 1. Abschnitt, Lieferung 2, Heft 2). Vol. I: The Early Period, 1975, second impression with corrections 1989. Vol. II: Under the Achaemenians, 1982. Vol. III (with F. GRENET): Zoroastrianism under Macedonian and Roman Rule, 1991.

BOYCE, M.: *Zoroastrianism: Its Antiquity and Constant Vigour*. Costa Mesa, California and New York 1992.

GNOLI, G.: "Zoroastrianism". *The Encyclopedia of Religion*, edited by M. ELIA-
DE, vol.15, New York 1987, 579–591.

HINNELLS, J.R.: *Zoroastrianism and the Parsis*. Ward Lock Educational, London
1981.

LOMMEL, H.: *Die Religion Zarathustras nach dem Awesta dargestellt*. Tübingen
1930, repr. Hildesheim/New York 1971.

NARTEN, J.: *Die Aməša Spəṇtas im Avesta*. Wiesbaden 1982.

NYBERG, H.S.: *Die Religionen des Alten Iran*. Leipzig 1938, repr. 1966.

Abbreviations

acc. = accusative

act. = active

adj. = adjective

adv. = adverb

aor. = aorist

Av. = Avestan

caus. = causative

comp. = comparative

conj. = conjunction

consec. = consecutive

dem. = demonstrative

denom. = denominative

desid. = desiderative

du. = dual

enclit. = enclitic

f., fem. = feminine

indecl. = indeclinable

indef. = indefinite

interrog. = interrogative

lit.= literally

m. = masculine

med. = middle

MP = Middle Persian

nom. = nominative

ntr. = neuter

part. = participle

pass. = passive

perf. = perfect

pers. = personal

plur. = plural

postp. = postposition

prep. = preposition

pres. = present

pron. = pronoun

rel. = relative

sg. = singular

subj. = subjunctive

subord. = subordinating

superl. = superlative

temp. = temporal

them. = thematic

Y = Yasna

Yt = Yašt